T0195807

teaching *and* counseling gifted girls

a
GIFTED CHILD TODAY *reader*

teaching
and counseling
gifted girls

edited by

susan k. johnsen

and

james kendrick

Routledge
Taylor & Francis Group

NEW YORK AND LONDON

First published 2005 by Prufrock Press Inc.

Published 2021 by Routledge
605 Third Avenue, New York, NY 10017
2 Park Square, Milton Park, Abingdon, Oxon OX14 4RN

Routledge is an imprint of the Taylor & Francis Group, an informa business

© 2005 by Taylor & Francis

Library of Congress Cataloging-in-Publication Data

Teaching and counseling gifted girls /
edited by Susan K. Johnsen and James Kendrick.
        p. cm.—(A gifted child today reader)
     ISBN 1-59363-169-3
     1. Gifted girls—Education—United States. 2. Gifted girls—Psychology. 3.
Sex differences in education—United States. 4. Educational equalization--
United States. I. Johnsen, Susan K. II. Kendrick, James, 1974– III. Series.

     LC3993.2.T43 2005
     371.95'082—dc22

                                                              2005019709

     ISBN 13: 978-1-59363-169-7 (pbk)

Contents

Overview

n 1992, the American Association of University
Women (AAUW) published a controversial
reported titled *How Schools Shortchange Girls*, in
which the authors argued that American schools
were not giving the same quality of attention to the
education of girls that they did to boys, thus perpet-
uating professional gender inequalities by turning
out better-prepared young men than women. This
seminal report expressed the realities of being a girl
in a modern American classroom, which was
fraught with issues regarding gender inequalities.
Many believed these issues had been dealt with during the second wave of feminism in the 1970s; however, a wake-up call to educators was sounded,
leading experts in the field to reexamine the implications school culture has on girls.

The report was caught in a crossfire of contro-
versy, with some heralding it as infallible proof that
girls were being cheated out of the educational
experiences necessary to earn a place in the highest
ranks of the workforce, while others argued that
the research evidence was not enough to support

the conclusions and that AAUW was absuing the findings to fit its preconcieved agenda.

Regardless of the report's faults and merits, *How Schools Shortchange Girls* was an important publication because it turned the public's attention toward important issues. Simply put, women continue to be underrepresented in many of society's most respected professions, particularly in the areas of science and technology, despite the fact that girls are well represented in gifted programs and make good grades throughout school, often better than their male peers. Research shows that the dreams and goals readily articulated by young gifted girls are often sacrificed in the adolescent years as girls succumb to society's messages about the importance of beauty over intellect, politeness over assertiveness, and domesticity over career success.

Gifted Girls in the Classroom covers some of the most important issues facing gifted and talented girls during their school years. In the first chapter, Jennifer L. Jolly sets the stage by offering an historical overview of the education of gifted girls, illustrating how the problems faced today are simply variations of problems the pioneers in the field of gifted education were addressing more than 80 years ago. In the next two chapters, Sally M. Reis then paints a detailed portrait of the world in which gifted girls live today and the various barriers to success that they face on a daily basis, both internal and external.

The next six chapters deal with gifted girls' social and emotional lives and various strategies teachers, counselors, and parents can use to help them navigate the tricky balancing act of maintaining emotional health while succeeding in the classroom and in a competitive, often unfair world. Leigh A. Rolnicki lays the groundwork describing the special needs gifted females have and why it is crucial that the adults in their lives recognize and help meet them, and Julianne Jacob Ryan explores how specialized counseling can aid gifted girls in coming out from behind the mask of conformity they create to hide their uniqueness. Thomas P. Hébert, Linda A. Long, and Kristie L. Speirs Neumeister offer the strategy of bibliotherapy to address gifted girls' social/emotional needs, including an annotated list of some biographies of eminent women that have proved particularly effective. Juanita Jo Matkins and Rhea Miles interviewed five women who have proved that women can "have it all" by being successful scientists, wives, and mothers, and their stories can be used to bolster girls' self-esteem and give them hope that their dreams can be fulfilled with hard work, determination, and careful planning. Similarly, the stories of "actualized" women related by Jan B. Jansen and Eleanor G. Hall can be used when talking to gifted girls about their goals and hopes for the future. Finally, M. Katherine Gavin and Sally M. Reis address eight specific strategies teachers can use to encourage girls who are gifted in mathematics, which could help balance the inequalities seen in scientific, mathematical, and technological professions.

Susan K. Johnsen
James Kendrick
Editors

The World of Gifted Girls

chapter 1

"The Woman Question"
*an historical overview
of the education of gifted girls*

by **Jennifer L. Jolly**

s the field of gifted education has evolved, so too has the role and treatment of gifted girls. From the inception of the field of gifted education in the early 20th century, gifted girls have faced challenges related specifically to their gender. During an era where women had just gained the right to vote, females were far from being considered an equal sex in both the classroom and the workforce and were treated accordingly.

Fast-forward nearly a century and the gender gap has partially closed in American society, allowing women greater opportunities in education and in the workforce. Examining the historical gains that gifted girls have made provides an interconnected narrative, so lingering issues regarding equal opportunity and treatment of gifted girls and women in their education and career choice can be viewed with the proper perspective.

Gifted education's earliest pioneer, Leta Hollingworth, recognized the barriers and challenges that women faced in society. Before beginning her work with gifted children, Hollingworth's early research had rejected the commonly held belief of the time period that women were less variable than men and thus less likely to obtain eminence. This was a bold position considering that her graduate advisor, E. L. Thorndike, was a major proponent of the variability theory. He stated,

> with the patent fact that in the great achievements of the world in science art, invention, and management, women have been far excelled by men. One who accepts the equality of typical representatives of the two sexes, must assume the burden of explaining this great difference in the high ranges of achievement. (cited in Hollingworth, 1914, p. 510)

Thorndike focused on physical factors, rather than environmental or societal factors, in order to explain a woman's seemingly limited variability. Hollingworth (1914) proposed that "Housekeeping and the rearing of children, though much commended to women as proper fields for the exploitation of their talents, are, unfortunately for their fame, not fields in which eminence can be attained. . . . Eminent housekeepers and eminent mothers *as such* do not exist" (p. 526).

Although, Hollingworth abandoned her early work on women's variability, she continued to champion reforms for women and advocate and give a voice to gifted girls (Hollingworth, 1990; Klein, 2003). Hollingworth's own graduate school experience was precipitated by her inability to gain work as a schoolteacher due to the fact that she was married. She was also a strong advocate for women's issues of the day, including birth control and the right to vote, often hosting teas and meetings in her own home. Hollingworth also recognized the unique challenges that gifted girls faced in American society, where seeking advanced degrees and entering the workplace was a rarity (Hollingworth; Klein).

After the development and publication of the Stanford-Binet in 1916, Hollingworth believed that scientifically based mental measures would alleviate the reliance on teachers' and parents' biased judgments when selecting and identifying gifted children for special classes, particularly girls. These judgments were considered circumspect for a variety of reasons. In a letter to Lewis Terman, another influential pioneer in the field of gifted education, Hollingworth wrote,

> I do not believe that teachers' judgments will supply a valid sampling. I believe that teachers (and people in general) tend to think the most intelligent; and that this results in the selection of girls who are personally attractive and pretty, at the expense of girls who are highly intelligent, but not so blest with desirable "feminine" qualities. . . . Surely there can be no question those parents and relatives are much more keenly interested in the abilities of male children. . . . During the past five years I have had a considerable number of voluntary requests for mental examination of children supposed by parents to be highly gifted, about twenty-five such requests in all. Only one of these was a request to examine a girl! (L. S. Hollingworth, personal communication to L. M. Terman, January 3, 1922)

The initial sample of Lewis Terman's longitudinal study begun in 1921 reflected a greater tendency to identify boys as gifted. However, he concluded that the findings directly supported the hypotheses that males are more variable than females, which in turn provided evidence that "exceptionally superior intelligence occurs with greater frequency among boys than girls" (Terman, 1925, p. 54). He reached this conclusion despite the fact that children in the sample were initially found through teacher recommendations, which generally favored boys.

Longitudinal data reported that boys did better in math and science, while girls did better in English and art. Over time, specialized abilities continued to show the same patterns: Girls reported abilities in art, writing, dramatics, household arts, and music, while boys reported abilities in mathematics, science, debating, and music ingenuity (Burks, Jensen, & Terman, 1930). As students moved into high school, trends began to change, with girls consistently receiving higher grades in all subject areas, including math and science. Seventy-five percent of the girls received A's in their school subjects, while the number for boys earning A's dropped to 45%. However, boys scored significantly higher than girls on achievement tests. College grade patterns similarly reflected high school grades except in the areas of science and public speaking (Burks et al.). Ninety percent of both boys and girls planned on attending college, and nearly half of those who graduated from college went on to postgraduate studies. A large portion of the noncollege graduates were women who chose to be housewives. However, Terman was most interested in seeing how women who had graduated from college would eventually combine a career and marriage (Burks et al.). Hollingworth (1926) called this dilemma

> "the woman question" how to reproduce the species and at the same time to work, and realize the work's full reward, in accordance with individual ability. This is a question primarily of the gifted, for the discontent with and resentment against women's work have originated chiefly among women exceptionally well endowed with intellect. (p. 349)

Gifted girls/women continue to struggle with this same "woman question": how to make significant contributions to their field while maintaining a family. However, research reveals that this struggle begins long before gifted women enter the workplace. Despite the gains women have made over the past eight decades, gifted girls still suffer the effects of sexism, discrimination, societal expectations, stereotypes, and differing self-concepts or perceptions when compared to boys (Olszewski-Kubilius & Turner, 2002). Gifted girls are given a variety of contradictory messages regarding their abilities and roles in society (Randall, 1997), and, in turn, they display contradictory behaviors themselves. In order to please others, they will hold back, rather than compete with boys, which is known is the "Horner Effect" or "Fear of Success" (Smutny, 1998).

While young, a gifted girl's intellect is cultivated and fostered; however, as gifted girls reach adolescence, other pressures such femininity, poise, and popularity supercedes intellect (Ryan, 1999). Although girls are choosing to take more rigorous math and science courses, they often do not follow through with careers that demand such knowledge and requisite skills. Additional research has reported a comparative number of boys and girls between the ages of 3 and 12 who tested above 180 IQ; however, the majority of highly accomplished or eminent individuals continue to be men (Silverman, 1997).

Hollingworth's (1914) belief that "the restriction of women to the mediocre grades of ability and achievement should be reckoned with by our educational systems" (p. 511) has only been partially realized. Schools and society, in general, still must work on the messages sent to girls and women about what careers are deemed appropriate. Nearly a century after Hollingworth's statement, gender continues to be the defining force for future talent development (Kerr & Nicpon, 2003).

References

Burks, B. S., Jensen, D. W., & Terman, L. M. (1930). *Genetic study of genius, Volume III: The promise of youth.* Stanford University, CA: Standford University Press.

Hollingworth, H. L. (1990). *Letta Stetter Hollingworth: A biography.* Bolton, MA: Anker.

Hollingworth, L. S. (1914). Variability as related to sex differences in achievement: A critique. *American Journal of Sociology, 19,* 510–530.

Hollingworth, L. S. (1926). *Gifted children: Their nature and nurture.* New York: Macmillan.

Kerr, B. A., & Nicpon, M. F. (2003). Gender and giftedness. In N. Colangelo & G. A. Davis (Eds.), *Handbook of gifted education* (3rd ed., pp. 493–505). Boston, MA: Allyn & Bacon.

Klein, A. G. (2002). *A forgotten voice: A biography of Letta Stetter Hollingworth.* Scottsdale, AZ: Great Potential Press.

Olszewski-Kubilius, P., & Turner, D. (2002). Gender differences among elementary school-aged gifted students in achievement, perceptions of ability, and subject preference. *Journal for the Education of the Gifted, 25,* 233–68.

Randall, V. (1997). Gifted girls—challenges they face: A summary of the research. *Gifted Child Today, 20*(4), 42–44.

Ryan, J. J. (1999). Behind the mask: Exploring the need for specialized counseling for gifted females. *Gifted Child Today, 22*(5), 14–17.

Silverman, L. K. (1997). *What we have learned about gifted children, 1979–1997.* Denver, CO: Gifted Development Center. (ERIC Document Reproduction Service No. ED428473)

Smutny, J. F. (1998). *Gifted girls*. Bloomington, IN: Phi Delta Kappa International.

Terman, L. M. (1925). *Genetic studies of genius. Volume I: Mental and physical traits of a thousand gifted children* Palo Alto, CA: Stanford University Press.

chapter 2

External Barriers Experienced by Gifted and Talented Girls and Women

by **Sally M. Reis**

> *I want my daughters to be beautiful, accomplished, and good; to be admired, loved, and respected; to have a happy youth, to be well and wisely married, and to lead useful, pleasant lives, with as little care and sorrow to try them as God sees fit to send. To be loved and chosen by a good man is the best and sweetest thing which can happen to a woman, and I sincerely hope my girls may know this beautiful experience.*
> —Louisa May Alcott, *Little Women*

ifted and talented females face conflicts between their own abilities and the social structures of their world. They confront both *external barriers* (i.e., lack of support from families, stereotyping, and acculturation in home, school, and the rest of society) and *internal barriers* (i.e., self-doubt, self-criticism, lowered expectations, and the attribution of success to effort rather than ability). Partial responsibility for the conflicts and barriers faced by talented women rests with the role confusion and ambivalence our society displays toward them and the barrage of conflicting messages that influence females throughout their lives. Examples of this ambivalence are plentiful, from teenage magazines to popular television. This is a longstanding issue. More than 50 years ago, when Pearl S. Buck originally published the novel *The Long Love*, she used the pseudonym of John Sedges, explaining, "I chose the name of John Sedges, a simple one, and masculine because men have fewer handicaps in our society than women have, in writing as well as in other professions."

The conflicts and barriers faced by gifted females involving their own abilities and the external pressures of their world have a direct impact on some of their most difficult decisions. These conflicts include the effects that challenging careers have on women's personal lives, which occur because talented women's multipotentiality often prohibits appropriate career counseling and decision making and helpful encouragement needed to succeed. Useful strategies for success are often obscured in a variety of mixed messages from women's families, friends, and society. Deborah Tannen (1990) explained the dilemma well:

> The different lenses of status and connection may once more work against women. Women are reluctant to display their achievements in public in order to be likable, but regarded through the lens of status, they are systematically underestimated, and thought self-deprecating and insecure. (p. 224)

These external barriers often interact with internal barriers, such as lowered expectations and career achievement, poor planning, lack of confidence in one's ability, and attributed success to effort rather than ability. These internal barriers are discussed in more detail in Chapter 3.

Current Statistics About Women, Work, and Accomplishments

Recent statistics highlight some of the problems facing talented women. These statistics, of course, tell only part of the story, and the story changes frequently. Since 1993, women have been losing ground to men in salary (Epstein, 1997). In 1979, women earned just 62.5 cents for every dollar earned by men, with the difference hovering at that level for a generation or so. A large number of antidiscrimination suits and an influx of women into the work force caused women to gain in salary benefits during the 1980s and early 1990s. By 1993, women earned 77 cents for every dollar earned by men. Epstein reported that, since then, equity in salaries has been in a downward spiral. In 1996, women earned only 75 cents for every dollar earned by men, and the figure has declined since then to 74 cents. Epstein believes that "because women as a group are lower on the company totem pole, they lose out on the prerogative to bestow bonuses, to distribute raises, and to hire, fire, transfer, and promote. Such power remains the preserve of men" (p. 35).

Epstein (1997) also reported only two female CEOs among the Fortune 500 companies and only five female CEOs among the next 500 companies. Golden West Financial chief executive Marion Sandler explained, "The people who are in a position of authority promote after their own image" (Epstein, p. 35). Carolyn Rogers, a vice president of J & W Seligman, agreed, indicating that the top echelons of business are "a men's club." Rogers further explained that men prefer to work with other men:

> It's not that they are intentionally overlooking women, it's just that who they've hung with, who they feel comfortable with, who they can communicate with, and who they trust are other men. And this kind of thing can often be a lot more important than sheer ability in determining the jobs women get. (Epstein, p. 35)

Women at Thirtysomething, a study released by the Office of Education (1991), included information on the educational careers and job market experiences of women who graduated from high school in 1972. Six surveys were conducted between 1972 and 1986 on a sample of more than 22,000 women. The study found that, as a group, women outperformed men academically at every level, had higher grade-point averages, completed degrees faster, and developed more positive attitudes toward learning. At the same time, a much higher percentage of women experienced genuine unemployment than men, regardless of what degree they earned. In only 7 of 33 occupations did women achieve pay equity with men.

Women who achieve high levels of success still experience blocks. The nonprofit Catalyst Group published a study entitled *Women and Corporate Leadership* (1996), in which half of the female executives interviewed about leadership reported that the major obstacles holding women back from top management positions were male stereotyping, preconceptions of women, and exclusion from informal networks of communication.

Another area in which statistics have not greatly changed for talented women is academe. According to the *Digest of Education Statistics* (Grant & Eiden, 1982), in the 1980–1981 academic year, 70% of full-time male faculty positions were tenured, as compared to 49.7% of female faculty positions. In 1994–1995, the tenure gap was virtually unchanged, at 71.3% for men and 50.3% for women. At many of our most prestigious universities and colleges, the percentage of women who reach the rank of full professor is still surprisingly low. The figures for 1997–98 indicate that, at Category 1 (doctoral granting) universities, the percentages of men who reach the level of full professor is 35.6% as compared to 5.7% for women. At the associate-professor level, a discrepancy still exists, with 20.3% of men reaching that level as compared to 8.7% of women (Schrecker, 1998, p. 34). At every rank and in every category, male professors earn more than female professors, even at the instructor and lecturer levels (Schrecker, p. 27). Many statistics across a range of areas suggest that barriers threaten accomplishment by women in general and talented women in particular (Reis, 1998, pp. 28–31):

- In 1978, two women headed Fortune 1,000 companies. In 1996, there were four women who headed Fortune 1,000 companies. A 1996 review of the 1,000 largest firms in the United States showed that women filled only 1% of the top five jobs in those corporations (60 out of 5,000 positions).
- Female musicians are drastically underrepresented in major orchestras in the world. Within the 21 highest budgeted orchestras in the United States, there are no female musical

directors or conductors in permanent positions. Of the total 1,530 pieces programmed in concerts for these orchestras, women composed only 3 pieces.

- Of the doctorates granted in mathematics in the mid-1990s, 78% were awarded to men, while 22% went to women.

- Of the doctorates granted in the physical sciences in the mid-1990s, the same percentages held, with 78% granted to men and 22% to women. Doctorates in engineering in the same time period reflected lower levels for women, with 88% granted to men and 11% to females.

- In the House of Representatives, women hold just 10.9% of the seats. In the Senate, women hold only 10% of the seats. Compare these to the percentages of women in the legislatures of the following countries (which have some of the best child-care leave policies in the world): Sweden, 40.4%; Norway, 39.4%; Finland, 33.5%; Germany, 26.2%; and South Africa, 25%.

Although some talented women have made inroads, many more have a long way to go in other occupations or fields of study.

Education and Financial Prospects

Since women more often pursue high school and associates (2 years of college) degrees, more men than women complete degrees at the bachelor's and graduate levels. A decreasing number of women are pursuing formal education for a number of reasons. Research by Reis (1998) indicated that, in most cases, fewer women pursue higher education because time- and energy-consuming relationships develop or because parents provided more emotional and financial support for their sons to complete degrees than for their daughters.

Not only are women's occupational patterns quite different from men's, so are their financial prospects in old age. After children, the single largest poverty group in our country is women over the age of 60. While the gap between earnings for women and men has decreased in recent years, the picture is much bleaker for older women, whose pensions are often a fraction of men's. The median annual pension benefit for newly retired women is $4,800, which is half the men's average of $9,600. Many factors appear to be detrimental to women in their retirement: their concentration in lower paid and part-time jobs with no retirement benefits, career interruptions to take care of family, and a tendency to avoid risky investments that may have big payoffs. According to Deborah Briceland-Betts, director of the Older Women's League, a national advocacy group, "retirement today is based on the male pattern of life, not the female," (Zaldivar, 1997, p. 10).

External Barriers

The importance of environmental variables on the development of gifted and talented females cannot be overstated. Almost from birth, females find themselves in a world of limiting stereotypes and other barriers to achievement. Research has identified external barriers that seem to influence negatively the development of talents and gifts in some females. These barriers include the role of parents, school, and the environment in general.

Parental Influences

The first set of external barriers gifted females face deals with childhood family issues and statistics, such as number and sex of siblings, birth order of siblings, and presence or absence of one or both parents. Other childhood issues include the parental attitudes toward having and raising girls as opposed to boys. Children usually learn the stereotypical behaviors of their sex at an early age and display particular behavior patterns and play preferences even during their preschool years (Blaubergs, 1980; Kirschenbaum, 1980; Paley, 1984). Research in the 1970s indicated that parents usually wanted a male child (Peterson & Peterson, 1973), and this trend may continue.

Once a child is born, various studies have reported that parents hold their children differently depending on whether they are girls or boys and purchase different toys that are stereotyped for each gender (Kuebli & Fivush, 1992; Schwartz & Markham, 1985). The contents and furnishings of girls' and boys' rooms have been found to be drastically different, with girls' rooms having more dolls and doll houses and boys' rooms having more vehicles, educational and art materials, and machines (Pomerleau, Bolduc, & Malcuit, 1990; Rheingold & Cook, 1975). Many studies have suggested that gender stereotyping in toys contributes to lower math and science scores for adolescent girls on achievement tests (Lummis & Stevenson, 1990; Olszewski-Kubilius, Kulieke, Shaw, Willis, & Krasney, 1990; Yee & Eccles, 1988). Patricia Casserly (1975), an early researcher in the area of gifted females, indicated that gifted girls were often frustrated because their parents would not buy them chemistry sets or construction sets as toys.

The educational levels and occupations of both father and mother and the type and level of parental aspirations for children's educational and occupational goals have also been shown to have an impact on the lives of talented females. *Shortchanging Girls, Shortchanging America,* a study conducted by the American Association of University Women (AAUW, 1991), included a poll of 3,000 students in grades 4–10 in 12 locations across the United States. The study found that, as girls get older, their self-esteem drops dramatically. Enthusiastic and assertive at ages 8 and 9, they begin to lose confidence in their abilities at ages 13 and 14 and emerge from high school with measurably lowered goals and future expectations. While 60% of the girls said they were happy with themselves in elementary school, 37% were still happy with themselves in middle school, and only 29% remained happy with themselves in high school. The self-reported reasons for the decline in self-esteem involving families and school experiences had the greatest impact on adolescents' self-esteem.

Parents often send contradictory messages that they want their daughters to get good grades in all subjects, but also to exhibit "appropriate" polite and even demure behavior, a clear finding derived from research (Reis, 1998). Stereotypical feminine behaviors often conflict with the personal attributes a gifted female needs to succeed. Some parents require—or, at a minimum, expect—their daughters to be polite, well-mannered, and consistently congenial. According to the stereotype, girls are not supposed to be too independent.

Mothers seem to have a particular influence on their gifted daughters. Recent research (Reis, 1998) found that talented girls with career-oriented mothers tended to develop a variety of talents and interests early in life and felt less conflict about growing up and becoming independent, autonomous women. Some gifted girls studied by Reis whose mothers had been at home, however, struggled with ambition and expressed conflicting feelings about work and home.

Lashaway-Bokina (1996) found similar results in her study of Latina American gifted females who had dropped out of high school. Many of the young women she studied were initially content to stay at home with their mothers and watch soap operas in the afternoon. These gifted females encountered confusing messages about their own future and their relationship with their mothers and regarded their own abilities and talent development with ambivalence. Their love for their mothers caused them to feel unsure about the development of their own talents. Their academic abilities, if developed, would lead to an unequivocally different life from the one in which they currently live and that their mothers would always live. Being different from their mothers and separating themselves in a number of ways from their families caused fear and tension in these young women. With time, however, some of them managed to reconcile their problems and return to high school. Few, however, have realized their academic potential and pursued post-secondary education.

Click, Click, Click: The Formation of Attitudes and Opinions

Like a camera in the brain, each time a child has an experience, a snapshot is embedded in her experiential base. Millions of snapshots produce attitudes, which, in turn, affect actions. Stereotypes abound in our society, from shampoo commercials and newspaper ads to the teen magazines our daughters read. Newspapers and news shows on television regularly feature photographs and feature stories about men in positions of authority. Children's books, television shows, and textbooks all present more men than women (Reis, 1998; Sadker & Sadker, 1994), and when women are presented, their appearances are usually stressed, rather than their talents, character, or value systems.

Girls and women are bombarded with unrealistic and superficial body images, and this stereotyping about weight and ideal proportions is a constant reminder to real women that they look less than ideal. Young women are encouraged to try to change themselves physically in order to gain happiness—to see supermodels as role models. Many talented girls are affected by the pressure to be attractive (Reis, 1998). Despite academic success, they consistently report that they seek and need approval from the males they date. One explained, "Males expect ideal body images, the impossible image. Many of us feel we will never measure up, and many guys make comments if we don't." (Reis, p. 135).

Each time a young girl turns on the television, reaches for a magazine, or participates in or overhears a conversation between friends, she is in the process of experiencing and being influenced by her social surroundings. The process begins at birth and continues throughout life, and the effects of environmental socialization are pervasive and overwhelming. Attitudes and opinions about what girls should look and act like come from family and friends, observations throughout life, television and other media, and print materials including books, magazines, and textbooks.

Popular girls and women's magazines reinforce gender stereotyping regularly. On the cover of a recent *YM* (*Young and Modern*) magazine was the photograph of a very slim, beautiful teenage girl, and the bullets of some of the stories inside included: "Total Love Guide: 100 Guys Dish the New Rules," "Kiss and Be Kissed: 26 Pucker-Up Pointers," "Dazzle Him: Hottest Date Clothes Ever," "31 Signs the Boy's Sweatin' You Bad," "Buff Your Bod: The Rock Goddess Way," and "12-Page Beauty Blitz and Major Makeovers: 10 Hot New Looks—Find the One For You."

Researchers and educators have made many suggestions for ways to eliminate or reduce the gender stereotypes that may prevent some gifted females from realizing their potential. However, we seldom witness the implementation of the widespread, comprehensive efforts necessary to ameliorate the effects of all of the "clicks" and social pressures that affect talent development in girls.

Stereotyping in School

Gender equity has still not been achieved in school textbooks and classroom experiences. In the past 10 years, a number of national reports and books have examined the impact of stereotyping on girls. *Failing at Fairness: How America's Schools Cheat Girls* (Sadker & Sadker, 1994) details differences in test scores, grades, classroom interaction, and numerous other areas, such as textbook inclusion of females. As an example, they cite *A History of the United States* (Boorstin & Kelley, 1992), a textbook in which fewer than 3% of the more than 1,000 pages focused on women.

The climates of elementary, middle, and high school, as well as college, have all been discussed as being responsible for changes in the attitudes of females relative to achievement in school. Research has indicated that boys more actively participate in school and receive more attention from teachers (Hall & Sandler, 1982; Jones, 1989; Krupnick, 1984, 1992; Sadker & Sadker, 1985, 1994). Some research indicates that a few male students receive more attention than all other students in math classes, and evidence exists that the amount of teacher attention given to girls is lowest in science classes (Handley & Morse, 1984; Jones & Wheatley, 1990; Shepardson & Pizzini, 1992). Reis and Kettle (1995) studied grouping in science and found that having mixed-gender groups usually resulted in boys dominating and conducting the hands-on science experiments. In groups of all females, however, the problem was eliminated and girls were able to participate fully.

Science and math classes, in particular, seem to include multiple examples of stereotyping. Lee and Marks (1992) reported the most blatant examples of stereotyping in chemistry. In another study, Tobin and Garnett (1987) found that boys conducted 79% of the science classroom demonstrations. These findings should raise questions about some of the suggestions made in research literature about how females may benefit from cooperative learning groups (Eccles, 1985; Fennema & Leder, 1990; Peterson & Fennema, 1985), as should new research about gifted females. For example, a study (Hernández Garduño, 1997) on gifted females who learned math in problem-solving situations found that females' attitudes toward math did not improve in class instruction based on the use of cooperative learning. Hernández Garduño found that mathematically talented girls in competitive, fast-paced classes scored higher in achievement tests than their counterparts in the cooperative learning groups. Qualitative data collected in the same study indicated that the talented girls who scored highest in math enjoyed competing with boys and liked trying to be the best. These mathematically talented girls were sometimes frustrated by the lack of challenge in some of the mixed-gender and single-sex cooperative learning groups. One participant explained, "It is interesting to work with others, but you get bored when you have to explain the same thing over and over and you want to go to the next problem. Sometimes it is better to be alone when you are solving problems" (p. 102).

Gavin (1996) obtained similar results studying gifted female college students who enjoyed academic competition and liked trying to be the best. Gavin cited two representative comments from gifted female math students she interviewed: "I enjoy competition and I enjoy being tested," explained one student, while another said, "I like to be at the top. . . . I like to be the best" (p. 479). In another recent research study on gifted females who scored at the very highest level on the math section of the SAT, O'Shea (1998) found similar results, confirming the research of both Gavin and Hernández Garduño (1997). The gifted young women O'Shea studied enjoyed both competition in math and competitive, fast-paced math classes. Therefore, it would be a mistake to confuse what may be appropriate for the majority of female students with what may be instructionally appropriate for talented females.

In another recent study of high-ability female students, Rizza (1997) found support for the research conducted by Hernández Garduño regarding the need for talented females to work alone. Rizza's research found that "solitary learning" was necessary when gifted female high school students pursued challenging academic work. Although these young women liked their friends a great deal and enjoyed socializing with them, most participants in the study wanted and needed to work alone when they had difficult academic tasks to complete.

Sexism in Colleges and Universities

Researchers have also found that university and college classrooms have numerous instances of silent sexism (Chamberlain, 1988; Glaser & Thorpe, 1986; Grant, 1988; Hall & Sandler,

1982; Rubin & Borgers, 1990), which create an atmosphere of inequality. Fay Ajzenberg-Selove (1994), a noted physicist, discussed this issue frankly in her autobiography:

> Are young women and young men treated equally in college? No, they are not. Overwhelmingly their science professors, particularly at the more prestigious universities, are males of an earlier era, an artifact of discrimination. Many of them, though consciously unaware of it, are uncomfortable with the women students in their classes. They are less likely to include women in class discussions and more likely to underestimate them. They can be intimidating and unpleasant. I believe that it is necessary that women faculty, as well as enlightened male faculty, discuss the importance of this problem with their other colleagues. It is very often the college which is at fault if a woman fails to pursue her scientific interests. And I believe that gender discrimination is a matter of still greater importance in graduate school when relationships with older scientists, with future patrons, are first established—relationships that are critical to a scientist's entire career. (p. 221)

Problems of sex discrimination at the college and university level often involve the same issues found in elementary and secondary school (Sadker & Sadker, 1994). Both male and female faculty treat their students differently based on sex. Dr. Bernice Sandler, director of the Association of American Colleges Project on the Status and Education of Women (PSEW), indicated that this treatment subtly undermines women's confidence and academic ability, lowers their academic and educational expectations, inhibits learning, and generally lowers self-esteem. To explain why some women become discouraged in the college classroom, Hall and Sandler (1982) cited professors' overt behaviors such as disparaging, belittling, and crude remarks; obscene jokes; and comments about physical appearance or clothing. Their study found approximately 30 different types of subtle behaviors that all tended to reinforce men's confidence while undermining women's. Female students believe that both male and female faculty call on men more often, use their names more frequently, give men more time to answer, and show more respect in their consideration of the responses. By their actions, the professors provide more positive reinforcement for men's responses than women's.

Work in the Home

Another external barrier many females experience as they attempt to realize their potential is the burden of responsibilities they often shoulder at home. Both daughters and sons learn and watch as their mothers work out of the home, come home to do the majority of work, or both. A greater amount of work at home occurs when women enter relationships: "Marriage creates work, far beyond the apparent practical need, in order that work may create marriage" (Bateson, 1989, p. 123). Bateson's observations of the customs of work created in marriage have also been echoed by many talented women (Reis, 1998). Of course, exceptions exist. Some partners, husbands, and fathers work diligently at home and support their spouses, but many do not. Other sociologists concur. Hartmann (1981) compared statistics on different types of households and found that the presence of an adult male creates more work for a woman than the presence of a child under 10, even when the man believes himself to be sharing the housework equally.

One study (Beck, Kantrowski, & Beachy, 1990) indicated that women also face the issue of caring for aging parents, estimating that the average American woman will spend 17 years raising children and 18 years helping aged parents. These added responsibilities will occur because of increasing longevity in our elderly population and will certainly block opportunities for talent development in our most high-potential females.

The Interaction of External Barriers and Internal Barriers

Noble (1987, 1989), a clinical psychologist who focused on the problems of gifted females, summarized data obtained from interviews with her clients, as well as the results of a survey of 109 women who attended a conference on gifted women. These data and a review of the literature on gifted females indicated that many gifted females are unaware of, ambivalent about, or frightened by their potential. She traced these findings to three sets of problems:

- *interpersonal obstacles* (e.g., rejection from family, teachers and peers; underestimation of abilities by families),
- *sociocultural barriers* (e.g., inadequate academic preparation, double messages), and
- *interpersonal factors* (e.g., self-doubt, disclaiming the label of giftedness).

These problems, defined in different ways, have also been cited in the literature by other researchers (Arnold, 1995; Callahan, 1979; Eccles, 1985; Hoffman, 1972; Hollinger & Fleming, 1988; Horner, 1972; Kerr, 1985; Reis, 1987, 1995a, 1995b, 1998).

A conflict may exist for gifted females because of the differences in value systems between men and women, such as the ethical sensitivities of women investigated by Gilligan (1982). Women seem to understand and recognize the importance of interpersonal relationships and connectedness in a way that causes them to understand the central role that relationships play in their lives. For gifted women, pursuing their own talents in a way that will enable them to nurture and realize their capabilities at the risk of taking time from their children or family may be a difficult, if not impossible, task (Reis, 1987, 1998).

Gifted and talented females face conflicts and barriers that exist between their own abilities and the social structure of their world. These conflicts include (a) women's inherent knowledge that society considers many challenging jobs to be more suited to the masculine psyche; (b) women's multiple talents that may prohibit appropriate career counseling and cause women to delay or avoid crucial decisions; and (c) a variety of mixed messages from their families, friends, and society that withhold or hide encouragement.

Jeanne Block (1982), a pioneer in gender research, believed that a fundamental task of the developing individual is the mediation between internal biological impulses and external cultural forces as they coexist throughout a person's lifespan. She further believed that the socialization process, defined as the internalization of values, appears to have differential effects on the personality development of males and females. Socialization, Block asserted, narrows women's options while broadening men's. Unfortunately, as girls get older, many of them learn that their perception of reality differs from the life experiences they encounter.

The most difficult conflict faced by the majority of gifted women studied by Reis (1998) revolves around the different experiences they face as young gifted girls who believe they can do everything. For them, a direct battle would be easier to fight than the subtle messages laden with guilt that they encounter later. Some young women today are in a more difficult position because they aren't able to take the hard-line stance against discrimination that their mothers' generation experienced 30 years ago. In previous decades, women could find some satisfaction in being strong—rebels of sorts—and they could appreciate gains when that behavior was recognized. These days, the obvious foes to women's talent development opportunities may be gone because of the success of the women's movement, but the reality of confronting more subtle obstacles and clear barriers still remains. Gifted females today are believed to have won the battle for equality and to have no more glass ceilings to break through. Unfortunately, they continue encountering them anyway. It's as if there aren't any real windmills to conquer because, in many cases, the windmills are far too hazy, and women really can't see them until they run right into them. A clearer understanding of the windmills and a plan for the future will enable more talented females to have opportunities to overcome them.

Recommendations for Addressing External Barriers

The following specific strategies have emerged from research on gifted girls, families, parents, teachers, and counselors. By implementing some strategies for each targeted group, attention can be given to various types of barriers encountered by talented girls and women.

Gifted and talented girls should:

- have exposure or personal contact with female role-models and mentors who have successfully balanced career and family;

- participate in discussion groups and attend panel discussions in which gifted and talented girls and women discuss the external barriers they have encountered;
- pursue involvement in leadership roles and extracurricular activities;
- participate in sports, athletics, and multiple extracurricular activities in areas in which they have an interest;
- discuss issues related to gender and success (e.g., family issues) in supportive settings with other talented girls; and
- participate in career counseling at an early age and be exposed to a wide variety of career options and talented women who pursue challenging careers in all areas.

Parents, teachers, and counselors should:

- form task forces to advocate for programming and equal opportunities and to investigate opportunities for talented, creative girls;
- spotlight achievements of talented females in a variety of different areas, encourage girls and young women to become involved in as many different types of activities, travel opportunities, and clubs as possible;
- encourage girls to take advanced courses in all areas, as well as courses in the arts, and reinforce successes in these and all areas of endeavor;
- ensure equal representation of girls in advanced classes;
- encourage relationships with other creative girls who want to achieve;
- maintain options for talented, creative girls in specific groups such as self-contained classes, groups of girls within heterogeneous classes, science and math clubs, or support groups; and
- consistently point out options for careers and encourage future choices but help girls focus on specific interests and planning for future academic choices, interests, and careers.

Parents should:

- become assertive advocates for the development of their daughter's interests and creative talents;

- maintain a proactive, supportive role to support their daughter's interests;
- provide career encouragement and planning;
- encourage experiences in museums, travel, and interaction with adults;
- develop interests;
- encourage participation in sports, competition, and extracurricular activities—teach their daughters that everybody loses sometime;
- monitor and discuss television viewing and media exposure—discuss the impact of magazines such as *YM*, *Cosmopolitan*, and other teen magazines that primarily stress appearance; and
- encourage creative action across domains—art, dance, cooking, science, etc.—and help focus interests.

Teachers should:

- provide equitable treatment and encouragement in a non-stereotyped environment;
- reduce sexism in classrooms and create an avenue for girls to report and discuss examples of stereotyping in schools;
- help creative, talented females appreciate and understand healthy competition;
- group gifted females homogeneously in math/science or within cluster groups of high-ability students in heterogeneous groups;
- encourage creativity in girls;
- use problem solving in assignments and reduce the use of timed tests and assignments within class periods by providing options for untimed work within a reasonable time frame;
- expose girls to other creative, gifted females through direct and curricular experiences (e.g., field trips, guest speakers, seminars, books, videotapes, articles, movies);
- provide educational interventions compatible with cognitive development and styles of learning (e.g., independent study projects, small-group learning opportunities, and so forth) and use a variety of authentic assessment tools such as projects and learning centers instead of just using tests;
- establish equity in classroom interactions; and

- provide multiple opportunities for creative expression in multiple modalities.

Counselors should:

- provide individualized, goal-oriented career counseling and maintain an interest in talented girls with high potential who need help in developing their creative talents;
- provide group counseling sessions for gifted and talented girls to discuss issues such as lack of encouragement from parents and peers;
- encourage participation in honors and Advanced Placement courses and in extracurricular activities and summer and out-of-school programs such as college science and math classes;
- sponsor conferences, workshops, and symposia for and about gifted, creative women for talented girls and their parents;
- establish support groups with a network of same-sex peers;
- contact parents when highly creative girls begin to seem confused about abilities, aspirations, or careers;
- provide a variety of career counseling and exposure opportunities;
- provide information about societies, Web pages, and resources that encourage and support gifted girls and women; and
- encourage selection of specific areas of creative pursuit.

References

Ajzenberg-Selove, F. (1994). *A matter of choices: Memoirs of a female physicist.* Brunswick, NJ: Rutgers University Press.

American Association of University Women (AAUW). (1991). *Short-changing girls, shortchanging America: A call to action.* Washington, DC: The American Association of University Women Educational Foundation.

Arnold, K. (1995). *Lives of promise: A fourteen-year study of achievement and life choices.* San Francisco: Jossey-Bass.

Bateson, M. C. (1989). *Composing a life.* New York: Plume.

Beck, M., Kantrowski, B., & Beachy, L. (1990, July 16). Trading places. *Newsweek,* 48–54.

Blaubergs, M. S. (1980). Sex-role stereotyping and gifted girls' experience and education. *Roeper Review, 2,* 13–15.

Block, J. H. (1982). *Sex role identity and ego development.* San Francisco: Jossey-Bass.

Boorstin, D., & Kelley, B. M. (1992). *A history of the United States.* Englewood Cliffs, NJ: Prentice Hall.

Callahan, C. M. (1979). The gifted and talented woman. In A. H. Passow (Ed.), *The gifted and talented* (pp. 401–423). Chicago: National Society for the Study of Education.

Casserly, P. L. (1975). *An assessment of factors affecting female participation in advanced placement programs in mathematics, chemistry, and physics.* Report of National Science Foundation (Grant GY–11325). Princeton, NJ: Educational Testing Service.

Catalyst Group. (1996). *Women and corporate leadership.* New York: Author.

Chamberlain, M. K. (Ed.). (1988). *Women in academe: Progress and prospects.* New York: Sage.

Eccles, J. S. (1985). Why doesn't Jane run? Sex differences in education and occupational patterns. In F. D. Horowitz, & M. O'Brien (Eds.), *The gifted and talented: Developmental perspectives* (pp. 251–295). Washington, DC: American Psychological Association.

Epstein, G. (1997, December). Low ceiling: How women are held back by sexism at work and child-rearing duties at home. *Barron's, 35–36.*

Fennema, E., & Leder, G. (Eds.). (1990). *Mathematics and gender.* New York: Teachers College Press.

Gavin, M. K. (1996). The development of math talent: Influences on students at a women's college. *Journal of Secondary Gifted Education, 7,* 476–485.

Gilligan, C. (1982). *In a different voice: Psychological theory and women's development.* Cambridge, MA: Harvard University Press.

Glaser, R. D., & Thorpe, J. S. (1986, January). Unethical intimacy: A survey of sexual contact and advances between psychology educators and female graduate students. *American Psychologist, 40,* 43–51.

Grant, L. (1988, July/August). The gender climate of medical schools: Perspectives of women and men students. *Journal of the American Medical Women's Association, 43,* 109–110.

Grant, W. V., & Eiden, L. J. (1982). *Digest of education statistics.* Washington, DC: U.S. Government Printing Office.

Hall, R., & Sandler, B. (1982). *Classroom climate: A chilly one for women?* Washington, DC: Project on the Status and Education of Women, Association of American Colleges.

Handley, H. M., & Morse, L. W. (1984). Two-year study relating adolescents' self-concept and gender role perceptions to achievement attitudes toward science. *Journal of Research in Science Teaching, 21,* 599–607.

Hartmann, H. I. (1981). The family as the locus of gender, class, and political struggle: The example of housework. *Journal of Women in Culture and Society, 6,* 366–394.

Hernández Garduño, E. L. (1997). *Effects of teaching problem solving through cooperative learning methods on student mathematics achievement, attitudes toward mathematics, mathematics self-efficacy, and metacognition.* Unpublished doctoral dissertation, University of Connecticut, Storrs.

Hoffman, L. (1972). Early childhood experiences of women's achievement motive. *Journal of Social Issues, 28,* 129–155.

Hollinger, C. L., & Fleming, E. S. (1988). Gifted and talented young women: Antecedents and correlates of life satisfaction. *Gifted Child Quarterly, 32,* 254–260.

Horner, M. (1972). Toward an understanding of achievement-related conflicts in women. *Journal of Social Issues, 28,* 157–176.

Jones, M. G. (1989). Gender issues in teacher education. *Journal of Teacher Education, 40,* 33–38.

Jones, M. G., & Wheatley, J. (1990). Gender differences in teacher-student interactions in science classrooms. *Journal of Research in Science Teaching, 27,* 861–874.

Kerr, B. A. (1985). *Smart girls, gifted women.* Columbus: Ohio Psychology Press.

Kirschenbaum, R. J. (1980). Combating sexism in the preschool environment. *Roeper Review, 2,* 31–33.

Krupnick, C. G. (1984). *Sex differences in college teachers' classroom talk.* Unpublished doctoral dissertation, Harvard University, Cambridge, MA.

Krupnick, C. G. (1992). Unlearning gender roles. In K. Winston & M. J. Bane (Eds.), *Gender and public policy: Cases and comment.* Boulder, CO: Westview Press.

Kuebli, J., & Fivush, R. (1992). Gender differences in parent-child conversations about past emotions. *Sex Roles, 27,* 683–98.

Lashaway-Bokina, N. (1996). *Gifted, but gone: High ability, Mexican-American, female dropouts.* Unpublished doctoral dissertation, University of Connecticut, Storrs.

Lee, V. E., & Marks, H. M. (1992). Who goes where? Choice of single-sex and coeducational independent secondary schools. *Sociology of Education, 65,* 226–253.

Lummis, M., & Stevenson, H. W. (1990). Gender differences in beliefs and achievement: A cross-cultural study. *Developmental Psychology, 26,* 254–263.

Noble, K. D. (1987). The dilemma of the gifted women. *Psychology of Women Quarterly, 11,* 367–378.

Noble, K. D. (1989). Counseling gifted women: Becoming the heroes of our own stories. *Journal for the Education of the Gifted, 12,* 131–141.

Office of Education. (1991, Fall). Women at thirtysomething. *OERI Bulletin,* p. 8.

Olszewski-Kubilius, P., Kulieke, M. J., Shaw, S., Willis, G. B., & Krasney, N. (1990). Predictors of achievement in mathematics for gifted males and females. *Gifted Child Quarterly, 34,* 64–71.

O'Shea, M. M. (1998). *Characteristics of high ability women who achieve in the 95th percentile on the quantitative section of the scholastic achievement test.* Unpublished doctoral dissertation, University of Connecticut, Storrs.

Paley, A. M. (1984). *Boys and girls.* Chicago: University of Chicago Press.

Peterson, P. L., & Fennema, E. (1985). Effective teaching, student engagement in classroom activities, and sex-related differences in learning mathematics. *American Educational Research Journal, 22,* 309–335.

Peterson, C. C., & Peterson, J. L. (1973). Preference for sex of off-spring as a measure of change in sex attitudes. *Psychology, 10(2),* 3–5.

Pomerleau, A., Bolduc, D., & Malcuit, C. (1990). Pink or blue: Environmental gender stereotypes in the first two years of life. *Sex Roles: A Journal of Research, 22,* 359–367.

Reis, S. M. (1987). We can't change what we don't recognize: Understanding the special needs of gifted females. *Gifted Child Quarterly, 31,* 83–89.

Reis, S. M. (1995a). Talent ignored, talent diverted: The cultural context underlying giftedness in females. *Gifted Child Quarterly, 39,* 162–170.

Reis, S. M. (1995b). Older women's reflections on eminence: Obstacles and opportunities. *Roeper Review, 18,* 66–72.

Reis, S. M. (1998). *Work left undone: Compromises and challenges of talented females.* Mansfield Center, CT: Creative Learning Press.

Reis, S. M., & Kettle, K. (1995). Unpublished evaluation report, Neag Center for Gifted Education and Talent Development, Storrs, CT.

Rheingold, H. L., & Cook, K. V. (1975). The content of boys' and girls' rooms as an index of parent behavior. *Child Development, 46,* 459–463.

Rizza, M. (1997). *Exploring successful learning with talented female adolescents.* Unpublished doctoral dissertation, University of Connecticut, Storrs.

Rubin, L. J., & Borgers, S. B. (1990). Sexual harassment in universities in the 1980s. *Sex Roles, 23*, 397–411.

Sadker, M., & Sadker, D. (1985). Sexism in the schoolroom of the '80s. *Psychology Today, 19*, 54–57.

Sadker, M., & Sadker, D. (1994). *Failing at fairness: How America's schools cheat girls.* New York: Macmillan.

Schrecker, E. W. (Ed.). (1998, March/April). Doing better: Annual report on the economic status of the profession, 1997–1998. *Academe, 84*(2), 14–103.

Schwartz, L. A., & Markham, W. T. (1985). Sex stereotyping in children's achievements. *Sex Roles, 12*, 157–170.

Shepardson, D., & Pizzini, E. (1992). Gender bias in female elementary teachers' perceptions of the scientific ability of students. *Science Education, 76*, 147–153.

Tannen, D. (1990). *You just don't understand me: Women and men in conversation.* New York: Ballantine Books.

Tobin, K. G., & Garnett, P. J. (1987). Gender related differences in science activities. *Science Education, 71*, 91–103.

Yee, D., & Eccles. J. (1988). Parent perceptions and attributions for children's math achievement. *Sex Roles, 19*, 317–334.

Zaldivar, R. A. (1997, November 30). In retirement, women face gender gap. Knight-Ridder Newspapers. *The Hartford Courant*, p. A1, A10.

chapter 3

Internal Barriers, Personal Issues, and Decisions Faced by Gifted and Talented Girls and Women

by Sally M. Reis

> *It is obvious that the values of women differ very often from the values which have been made by the other sex. Yet, it is the masculine values that prevail.*
> —Virginia Woolf (1957)

esearch with gifted and talented females has revealed a number of internal barriers, personal priorities, and decisions that have consistently emerged as the reasons that many either cannot or do not realize their potential. These barriers, priorities, and personal decisions were identified in hundreds of interviews conducted with girls and women at various stages across the lifespan and in a variety of occupations (Reis, 1998). Of course, not all gifted women experience the same dilemmas and decisions, but commonalities have been found in research on this population. These include dilemmas about abilities and talents; personal decisions about family; and decisions about duty and caring (putting the needs of others first) as opposed to nurturing personal, religious, and social issues. It is difficult, if not impossible, to discuss gifted girls without discussing gifted women because many young gifted girls believe that they can "do it all" or "have it all," while many older gifted females have learned that they cannot.

These personal issues occur across the lifespan. Some affect the girls in the primary grades, and some are only apparent to women in their college or graduate school years. What is essential to note is that most of the personal issues discussed in this chapter have been resolved by older talented women studied by Reis (1995). The age of 50 seems to be a key age for understanding and resolving most of the dilemmas that face many gifted women, although some found solutions earlier. It is also important to understand that some of these dilemmas cannot be resolved to the satisfaction of everyone involved. Rather, some dilemmas end with changes in a woman's life, such as the maturation of her children, the dissolution of a relationship, the reemergence of other relationships, or a change in environments at work or home.

Internal Barriers, Personal Issues, and Decisions

Consistent trends found in interviews with many young gifted women indicate that they grew up believing that they did not face the barriers their mothers and grandmothers encountered (Reis, 1998). As they grew older, many encounter both internal and external barriers. When and how do women learn about the barriers that affect achievement?

Hollinger and Fleming (1984) found no sign of recognition of internal barriers affecting accomplishment in women in 29% of the 284 gifted adolescents they studied. Recent research (Reis, 1998) has indicated, however, that the conflicts and barriers become more apparent as gifted girls mature and face decisions at critical junctures in their lives. In fact, the intersection of these factors—ability, age, career choice, and personal decisions related to marriage and children—may result in additional internal barriers.

Can't I Do It All?

In an interview conducted almost 20 years ago, a gifted teenage girl named Maria became angry with questions about perceived barriers she might confront in her future. Maria indicated that she faced no barriers, the women's movement had paved the road, and she could certainly have it all. She explained that her dreams included a road map for her future: an education at a first-rate women's college, a graduate degree, a university position teaching to support her while she wrote the great American novel, a husband, and children.

When Maria was interviewed almost 20 years later, she had finished her undergraduate degree and had fallen in love during college. She had not gone to graduate school, but had financially and emotionally supported her husband, whom she loved deeply, in his pursuit of his career. She spoke about his talents in glowing terms and showed me photographs of their young child who was the joy of her life. When asked about her plans for graduate school and her writing, she paused and said, "Oh, today I am much more realistic about my goals. I try to get through the week and take care of my family. I also am devoted to my husband's dreams." She explained quietly, "You know, I bought the whole superwoman thing, but it's just not right to put my own needs ahead of the needs of my child and my husband. He has such dreams about his work." Instead, she deferred her own dreams, and only time, perhaps decades, will tell if they will reappear again or simply change.

Young girls often believe they can do anything and everything. Then, they begin to encounter the subtle messages laden with guilt later in their life. Many gifted and talented women begin to feel that being ambitious is synonymous with being selfish. Even those women who have made it to the pinnacle of their field suffer from decisions about priorities. In an article about elite female Olympic athletes, Martha Ludwig (1996) painted a poignant portrait:

> Many female Olympic athletes attempt to juggle the pressures of competition along with a career, a romantic relationship, and parenthood. In spite of the assumed sociological strides made toward equality between women and men in the 1980s and 1990s, high-performance female athletes continue to encounter the obstacles of traditional gender roles. (p. 31)

Female Olympic athletes reported to Ludwig (1996) that their spouses often did not provide enough support at home. These women carried the primary responsibility as wife, mother, homemaker, career person, and elite athlete. "Many female athletes face the consequences of identity overload and must struggle to determine the priorities and balance of daily life within a nonsupportive environment. Gender continues to make a difference" (p. 32). Ludwig also found that many of the elite female athletes delay relationships and childbirth, rather than shoulder these responsibilities alone.

Some of these personal issues described in this article affect both young girls and older women. It is difficult to pinpoint exactly when many of these issues surface in younger girls and women, but some research indicates that many of the difficult personal choices and dilemmas facing younger females are resolved as women age (Reis, 1998). With reflection, discussion, supportive friends and partners, and the right environment, younger girls and women can also address and perhaps resolve many of the difficult choices they face. These discussions can be guided by an examination of the critical personal issues they face and personality factors they possess.

Gilligan's Concept of a Different Ethic of Caring

Many gifted and talented females face a difficult, almost unsolvable, dilemma: How to put their own talents first when their entire life had been based upon the importance of relationships and the tacit belief that women always put *others* first. According to Gilligan (1982), women not only define themselves in a context of human relationships, but judge themselves in terms of their ability to care for others. Historically, women have nurtured, taken care of, and helped their children and spouses. They have developed networks of relationships that are vital to them. Women may be more concerned than men about relationships and express a greater need for successful ones.

Most of the gifted and talented women Reis (1998) studied understood that, if they developed their own talents, there would be an impact on those they loved. They often were frustrated with their own inability to resolve the need to do two things: support, care for, and maintain relationships with those they loved while simultaneously pursuing a talent or gift to its fullest level. Many only resolved their frustrations about their inability to pursue their own talents at a later age.

Gilligan (1982) found that a woman's sense of integrity is entwined with an *ethic of care*, which for some is confused with either seeking or needing approval from loved ones. She explained that making the distinction between helping and pleasing frees the activity of care giving from needing approval from others. At that point, responsibility can become a self-chosen anchor of personal integrity and strength.

The ethic of care described by Gilligan, accompanied by women's belief in the importance of relationships, has been found to be the single greatest issue to address for gifted females who also have their own unique dreams and aspirations for important work (Reis, 1998). Many gifted women in their 20s, 30s, and 40s experience guilt over what they want to do for themselves and what they believe they should do for their families and for those they love. Most struggle with finding time to do their own work and often put their work off until they have met all family obligations. As a result, they often have little time left for their own creative work. As one of the artists studied by Kirschenbaum and Reis (1997) explained, personal work is only possible

> when my life is in order, the kids are happy, dinner is cooking, the house is clean, the laundry is caught up, and there's a semblance of calm in the household, it just seems like ideas flow. I can sit down and write poetry just like that. I can sit at the computer and turn out two or three pages of a screenplay.

Creation of a Sense of Self and a Feminine Identity

One of the older gifted women Reis (1998) interviewed was most eloquent as she explained her search to find herself.

> I was never called by my own name until my husband died. As a young girl, I was always Arthur's daughter. When I married, I was Charlie's wife. When I had children, I was Sarah and David's mother. It was only after

my children grew up and my husband died that I was recognized as Berice and called by my own name. I realized I had lost my sense of self as a young girl and only regained it as an older woman.

Most young girls in elementary and middle school do not have an *understanding of self.* They begin to learn who they are in high school and college, only to have their sense of self waver as they become involved in a relationship. A sense of self is critical to the development of talent in women. Profound changes in a woman's personal life can alter her sense of self; an early marriage and a resulting name change, for example, may shift or erode it. If women marry at young ages and have children early in the marriage, they often have little or no time to regain their sense of self. Reis (1998) found that gifted women who marry in their late 20s or early 30s are able to establish a stronger sense of self and are more often able to maintain their understanding of and belief in self than if they marry earlier.

The Development of Self-Efficacy

According to Bandura (1986), *self-efficacy* is a person's judgment about his or her ability to perform a particular activity. He found a positive relationship between self-efficacy beliefs and academic performance. Sources for increasing self-efficacy include past performances, the vicarious experiences of observing models who are like yourself, verbal persuasion, and physiological clues (Bandura). Because of the external and internal barriers they confront in life, many gifted females do not have the opportunities to develop self-efficacy. They receive less verbal persuasion from their parents and friends, observe fewer role models, and produce less creative work.

Multipotentiality

Women who demonstrate multipotentiality usually have an eagerness to learn and a thirst for knowledge (Ehrlich, 1982); receive uniformly high scores across ability and achievement tests (Sanborn, 1979); are involved in multiple educational, vocational, and leisure interests at comparable intensities; and have complex

personality factors. Women with high potential and multiple interests often have multiple academic, career, and leisure possibilities,
and these choices constitute *multipotentiality*. For some, having
many choices is beneficial because they result in a variety of
options. Others, however, often cannot find their niche, make it
on their own, or choose a vocational path (Fredrickson, 1979,
1986; Jepsen, 1979; Kerr, 1981; Marshall, 1981; Sanborn; Schroer
& Dorn, 1986). Many women with multipotentiality find decision making difficult since it is not possible to do all that they
would like to do and are capable of doing.

Personal factors may also affect females who demonstrate
multipotentiality. Perrone and Van Den Heuvel (1981) found
that multipotentiality may lead students to commit to a career
too quickly in order to reduce tensions caused by a vast array of
competing options. Other multipotential women may have
career choices externally imposed on them by their parents or
teachers, who believe they know what's right for them
(Silverman, 1993). Still others may simply become engrossed in
a single subject area at a very early age and waver little from this
choice, deliberately closing doors to many unexplored possibilities in order to eliminate the likelihood of any unwanted confusion (Marshall, 1981; Silverman). A connection between
personality attributes and the "overchoice syndrome" seems to
exist (Clark, 1992; Schmitz & Galbraith, 1985). The areas of
self-exploration, self-criticism, intellectual maturity, and the
presence of complex value systems all interact with multipotentiality. Women with a wide range of personality characteristics
and perspectives often have a difficult time understanding
themselves and making appropriate choices for career and
advanced training.

The Development of Resilience

Theories about resilience attempt to explain achievement
among those who are subjected to negative psychological and
environmental situations. Rutter (1987) defined *resilience* as
"the positive role of individual differences in people's responses
to stress and adversity" (p. 316).

Resilience is not a fixed attribute in individuals. The successful negotiation of psychological risks at one point in a person's

life does not guarantee that the individual will react positively to other stresses when situations change. The gifted women Reis (1998) studied used successful resilience strategies and achieved, while others of similar ability who faced similar problems did not. These gifted artists, scientists, authors, politicians, activists, and scholars took control of their own learning. Determination, insight, independence, initiative, humor, and creativity characterized their lives. A famous female composer in a study of older talented women explained that music appreciation and music history books were filled with male composers and it was time for more females to enter those pages (Reis, 1995).

Several factors contributed to the development of resilience. Strong family and relationship ties, friendships with other women and men, love of work, and a passion to continue doing what they love are all attributes of resilient gifted females (Reis, 1998). Likewise, the realization that defeat sometimes provides an opportunity for learning to occur also contributes to developing resilience. For example, a prominent college president explained that that she understood that criticism from faculty, students, and the press was a "part of the territory" when she accepted the position. She expected criticism and regarded it as the predecessor to positive action (Reis).

Fear of Success or Fear of Not Finding a Partner Who Celebrates Your Success

Some researchers believe *fear of success syndrome*, first introduced by Horner in 1970, is a key factor in understanding the problems facing gifted females. Fear of success may cause some females to believe that they will be rejected by their peers or appear undesirable to the opposite sex if they are too competent or successful. Horner explained that many capable young women change their plans to accommodate a less ambitious, more traditionally feminine role.

Sassen (1980) reexamined success anxiety in women, finding that the climate of competition may result in anxiety instead of success for some women. She suggested that this anxiety might be a reflection of an essentially female way of constructing reality and called for a way to restructure society and institutions so that competition is not the only avenue to success.

However, Reis' research with women in their late 20s, 30s, and older indicates that these women do not fear success, but often regard it with ambivalence. This ambivalence occurs not because they fear rejection from either peers or individuals in whom they may have a romantic interest, but rather because they don't desire the trappings that may accompany success. These trappings include overexposure in a public life, an inability to balance success with time for family and other loved ones, an overt dislike of the perceived competition that may be necessary to achieve success, and a strong dislike of the types of behavior that may become necessary to maintain success.

Some ambivalence about success may affect women at all levels of accomplishment, from the most eminent to those who are beginning their rise to success. Even female Olympic contenders experience fear of success. In a study of Olympians, Ludwig (1996) found fear of both success and failure, indicating that fear of failure is manifested in a similar manner by both men and women, but that fear of success is primarily a female issue. "Fear of success for women seems to initiate from a cognitive belief system that sometimes becomes an insurmountable obstacle to success" (p. 31).

Fear of success at an early age, however, may lead to a change in confidence in one's ability and can have devastating effects if it occurs during college or graduate school. Results in a study of high school valedictorians by Arnold (1995) found that female students who had done well in high school lost confidence in their ability after a few years of college. In their second year of college, the female valedictorians lowered their assessments of their intelligence. The effects of this loss of self-confidence can influence the rest of a young woman's life if it causes her to change college plans, goals for graduate study, or choice of partner or career. Arnold's conclusions suggest gender differences in intellectual self-esteem of talented females who realize that their career decisions will interact, perhaps negatively, with both their relationships and motherhood.

Absence of Planning or Poor Planning

Another issue affecting young talented females is their inability to plan for the future in a realistic way. Many young women ignore or are unaware of the economic reality that most will have to work their entire lives to support themselves, their families, or both. Males, on the other hand, grow up with the understanding that they will have to work for a lifetime; thus, they select more appropriate long-range career goals.

Because some women do not learn to plan, they often have not thought about how they might juggle a marriage, career, family, graduate school, and advanced study. Some talented girls have unrealistic beliefs that they can go through college and graduate school, begin a career, and then interrupt that career to marry and have children without consequence to their career choices and professional advancement (Reis, 1998). Parents and teachers must consider planning as a way of working with young gifted females to help them establish clear goals that will guide them if they should become involved in a relationship and consider deferring their own dreams. Talented young women have to learn that planning for themselves is essential and not a selfish act. In 1898, Charlotte Perkins Gilman wrote about planning in *Women and Economics*, "Where young boys plan for what they will achieve and attain, young women plan for *whom* they will achieve and attain" (p. 18). Planning for one's education and personal dreams can provide the tools necessary to enable talented females to have choices, as well as to understand the ramifications of decisions to discontinue an education or change a career plan because of a relationship.

Hiding Abilities, Doubting Abilities, and Feeling Different

Buescher and his associates (1987) studied gifted adolescents and found that, while 15% of boys hide their abilities in school, 65% of girls consistently hide theirs. Reis (1998) found that gifted girls do not want to be considered different from their friends and same-age peers. Indeed, a tendency exists for many females, regardless of age, to try to minimize their differences. For many gifted girls, however, the problem grows more difficult as they become women and their talents and gifts set them apart from their peers and friends. In school environments where academics take a back seat to athletics or other activities, the issue may be exacerbated.

Learning why females mask or hide their abilities is often critical to addressing the problem, and finding environments in which success is celebrated and individual differences are respected is crucial.

In addition to hiding abilities, some gifted and talented females begin to doubt that they really have abilities. If women do not recognize their potential, they usually will not fulfill it. In a 50-year study of female graduates who attended a school for gifted students in New York City (Walker, Reis, & Leonard, 1992), three out of four women did not believe in their superior intelligence, and most of them selected mediocre and gender-stereotypic jobs, often due to pressure from parents and teachers.

It is difficult to live in a community when you either feel or are different. Wanting to spend large blocks of time doing their work instead of more gender-acceptable tasks such spending time with friends and being involved in community service often sets older talented women apart. These women report that they are constantly asked why they can't be happy with their life. A congresswoman in a study of older eminent women indicated that her female friends asked her in amazement each time she ran for re-election, "Why do you do this to yourself?" (Reis, 1998). An unfortunate by-product of a creative productive life is the reality of few friendships. Many talented women have indicated that they did not have enough time for friends (Reis). For some women, at age 50 and over, as other relationships ended and children grew up and moved out, some patterns of friendship were renewed and the feelings of separation diminished. But, the feelings of being different seldom left.

The Impostor Syndrome

A related issue occurs when females achieve high levels of success: the *great impostor syndrome* (Clance, 1985; Clance & Imes, 1978). This syndrome describes a low sense of self-esteem that occurs when females attribute their successes to factors other than their own efforts and see their outward image of a bright successful achiever as being undeserved or accidental. "I was lucky," "I was in the right place at the right time," "I really didn't do as well as it seems," and "I had a lot of help" are all statements made by talented females complimented on their successes. This reaction to compliments and success does not seem to affect males to the same degree. More talented males of all ages have been found to attribute their achievements to their own efforts, saying "thank you" when they are complimented, while more girls attribute their accomplishments to external forces and not to themselves.

Females tend to attribute their successes to effort or external factors such as luck, while failures are explained as internal faults or the result of their lacking certain abilities. On the other hand, males attribute their success to their own capabilities and failure to external factors. Attribution theory indicates that the masculine attribution pattern is more likely to provide a greater motivation for performance than the feminine pattern. Weiner (1986) found that attributions can influence emotions, self-concepts, and subsequent behaviors.

In a research study conducted with high school valedictorians, Arnold (1995) found that, by the second year of college, over a quarter of the female high school valedictorians she studied had lowered their self-rankings of their intelligence, indicating that they were merely average in intelligence. This phenomenon did not occur with the male valedictorians, whose self-rankings remained consistent or actually improved. The women Arnold studied continued this pattern at graduation from college. None of the women placed herself in the highest category of intelligence, while men, in sharp contrast, steadily increased their self-ratings.

Some talented women actually begin to believe that they accomplished success because they fooled other people or that were successful due to having the right mentor, a happy disposition, or an act of chance. In some cases, this feeling of accomplishing success due to luck or chance has occurred because talented girls and women can often accomplish a great deal without the effort that is often required from their less-capable peers. If ability is high and less effort is warranted, many women begin to feel that they are lucky, rather than gifted. Self-reflection, discussion, and time are often necessary to overcome the great imposter syndrome. Supportive environments, counseling, and peer support are also important for understanding that success is attained in different ways.

Confusion About Effort and Ability

Linked to the great imposter syndrome is the difficulty experienced by many talented women in understanding the complex relationship between *effort* and *ability*. Most people believe that effort and ability are the reasons that they achieve or underachieve in school and life. According to attribution theory (Weiner, 1986), effort and ability are both internally perceived causes, and understanding the relationship between them is important. Many high-achieving students tend to attribute their successes to a combination of ability and effort and their failures to lack of effort. On the other hand, individuals who accept their own failure often attribute their successes to external factors such as luck and their failures to lack of ability.

Before the age of 10, children are usually unable to distinguish effort from ability. However, as they approach adolescence, they begin making a distinction, and gender differences emerge. Boys more often attribute their successes to ability and their failures to lack of effort, while girls often attribute their successes to luck or effort and their failures to lack of ability. The academic self-efficacy of young males is enhanced based on their belief in their ability. It is maintained during failures because of the young male's attribution of failure to lack of effort. The same does not appear to be true for young females. Girls may accept responsibility for failure, but not for success. Researchers believe that, although girls may perceive themselves to be bright, they interpret any failure quite negatively, believing that it is caused by lack of ability (Dweck, 1986).

Developing a strong belief in one's ability in the elementary and middle school years is important because, "by the end of elementary school, children's [perceptions] . . . of ability begin to exert an influence on achievement processes independent of any objective measures of ability" (Meece, Blumenfeld, & Hoyle, 1988, p. 521). Many gifted adolescent girls believe that possessing high ability means that they will achieve excellent grades without effort. Students often believe that, if they must work hard, they lack ability (Dweck, 1986). During adolescence, talented girls may move from self-confidence to self-consciousness and often have doubts about their ability (Reis, 1998).

Unfortunately, teachers often contribute to this confusion about effort and ability. As early as first grade, teachers tend to attribute boys' successes and failures to ability and girls' successes and failures to effort (Fennema, Peterson, Carpenter, & Lubinski, 1990). Teachers also contribute to confusion by stressing the time assigned for tasks or tests. Girls, all too often, learn that being fast equals being smart. This time pressure may be discouraging to girls who are often more reflective and may take longer to think than boys of similar intellectual potential.

Researchers have found that teachers' feedback about work is a better predictor for children's self-perceptions of their ability and effort than are other types of interactions with teachers or with peers (Pintrich & Blumenfeld, 1985). Seigle and Reis (1998) found that teachers still rate adolescent gifted females higher than gifted males on effort. Schunk (1984) found that children who initially receive feedback complimenting their ability, rather than feedback complimenting their effort, developed higher ability attribution, self-efficacy, and skills. This finding clearly indicates that parents and teachers should praise girls for their ability, thereby helping them come to understand that they have ability. It is also essential that young girls learn early about effort and understand that the most talented people expend a great deal of it to be successful at challenging pursuits.

Searching for Perfection

Perfectionism may be regarded as both a positive and negative influence in one's life. Hamachek (1978) viewed perfectionism as a manner of thinking about behavior and described two different types of perfectionism, normal and neurotic, that form a continuum of perfectionist behaviors. *Normal perfectionists* derive pleasure from the labors of effort and feel free to be less precise as the situation permits. *Neurotic perfectionists* are unable to feel satisfaction because they never seem to do things well enough. Hamachek identified six specific overlapping behaviors describing both normal and neurotic perfectionists: depression, a nagging feeling of "I should," shame and guilt feelings, face-saving behavior, shyness and procrastination, and self-deprecation.

Too many talented females spend their lives trying to be perfect. In addition to investing considerable energy in trying to be the best athlete, the best dancer, the best scholar, the best friend, and the best daughter, young girls and women often feel that they must also be slender, beautiful, and popular. This perfectionism is often a result of parental pressures, as well as pressures from the media, and a conscious or unconscious desire to try to make everyone happy. A perfectionism complex can cause talented women to set unreasonable goals for themselves and strive to achieve at increasingly higher levels. It also can cause them to strive for impossible goals and spend their lives trying to achieve perfection in work, home, body, children, and other areas.

In a study on perfectionism in gifted adolescents in a middle school, Schuler (1997) found that perfectionism can be viewed as a continuum with behaviors ranging from healthy/normal to unhealthy/dysfunctional. Order and organization, support systems, and personal effort were the factors that impacted the healthy perfectionists. All of the healthy female perfectionists had been aware of their perfectionist tendencies since they were young, with their first memories related to school activities. While this need for order was pervasive among these gifted girls, they felt supported by their families, friends, and peers. They received encouragement to do their "personal best" academically and were told that mistakes were acceptable parts of learning. Their teachers considered the healthy female perfectionists responsible, cooperative, organized, considerate, and conscientious workers. On the other hand, concern over mistakes, perceived parental expectations, and perceived parental criticisms were the salient factors for the gifted unhealthy/dysfunctional female perfectionists. They possessed a fixation about making mistakes that resulted in a high state of anxiety. Their definitions of perfectionism focused on not making any errors.

The majority of the unhealthy female perfectionists worked to please others—teachers, peers, or parents. Unlike the healthy female perfectionists, they viewed their parents' perfectionism negatively and perceived parental expectations as demands to be perfect in everything they did. Comments such as, "Don't fail," "Do the best," "Where are the A's?," and "You should do better" were not interpreted as motivators, but as criticisms of their efforts, leading them to be highly critical of themselves and possess an intense concern over making mistakes.

The unhealthy female perfectionists were critical of themselves and of those they wanted to impress, especially a parent or other perfectionist peer. Their own inappropriate expectations added to the pressure they faced, and the consequences were self-doubts, procrastination, repeating work over and over, taking an exceedingly long time to complete tasks, and constant anxiety and worry.

Different Messages From Home and School

Many young girls have problems reconciling messages that have emerged from different environments. For example, if a teacher tells a girl to speak out in class, raise questions, and be assertive in pursuing her talents, this teacher's message may directly conflict with what this girl has been told at home. Parents often have strict guidelines about manners for their daughters at home, such as not being too aggressive and acting like "a young lady." However, looking cute, minding their manners, and being polite and ladylike may conflict with characteristics necessary for girls with high potential to evolve into successful women who make a difference.

To develop into successful women, smart girls need to challenge convention, question authority, and speak out about things that need change. The very characteristics found to be associated with older talented women (e.g., determination, commitment, assertiveness, and the ability to control their own lives) directly conflict with what some parents encourage as good and appropriate manners in their daughters (Reis, 1998). The manners taught to some daughters and sons are, of course, influenced by the culture in which we live. While not wanting to eliminate what is unique to each diverse culture, a discussion of some of the issues related to strict implementation of a code of manners and behavior for girls, as well as boys, is warranted.

Dabrowski (1967) is one of the few theorists whose personality theories have been applied to gifted individuals. Dabrowski believed that some people display supersensitivities or overexcitabilities in several areas: psychomotor (increased levels of physical activities), intellectual (increased levels of intellectual activities), sensual (expanded awareness), imaginational (high levels of imagination), and emotional (intensified emotions).

Talented young girls may experience some of these overexcitabilities, and they often have expanded awareness in the sensual, imaginational, and emotional areas. Too strict a behavior code may directly conflict with their emotional nature and could be difficult for parents to enforce and for children to obey. Parents who demand a certain behavior code at all times sometimes squelch the passion and the love of questioning and talking from their outgoing, spirited daughters. Parents and teachers should try to channel the overexcitability, determination, willfulness, or stubbornness they find in gifted girls to something positive, such as social action, improving some aspect of life, sports, hobbies, music lessons, or any personal interest area.

Unreal Expectations of Future Careers, or Part-Time Work for a Full-Time Future

Some young girls want to be doctors, lawyers, or scientists when they grow up, but don't know how to plan to achieve these goals. They may have no idea about the time commitment or the requirements involved in these careers. Many have not considered how they will integrate personal relationships with this process, and, if they fall in love, few are prepared to make decisions to enable them to have both challenging careers and satisfying personal lives. Instead, they often put the interests of the person they love ahead of their own.

In their study of women in a southern university, Holland and Eisenhart (1990) found that many of the women they studied viewed boyfriends as a source of prestige and romantic relationships as positive, normal, and desirable. However, women in this study also admitted to having difficulty with achieving a balance between their romantic relationship, work, academic classes, and peer involvement. Holland and Eisenhart found that, contrary to popular belief, women who fell in love did not lower their ambitions *because* they fell in love. Rather, they lowered their ambitions and *then* they fell in love. The enemy of ambition in some of these high-achieving young women was their own peer group of other women. Almost all of the women studied by Holland and Eisenhart gradually experienced a decline in their ambitions and their aspirations, pointing again to the importance of planning for gifted girls across their lifespans.

Because many talented young women lower their aspirations, they end up choosing less-demanding careers that they believe will enable them to marry or be involved in a committed relationship. Many leave work to raise their children and plan to reenter the workforce at a later time. To this end, they may choose not to pursue careers in math or science or they may decide to postpone their completion of advanced degrees in a professional career. Instead, they may select a more traditional female service career, such as teaching, medical technicians, secretarial, or childcare that they believe will enable them to leave and return to work when their children are older.

In the study of high school valedictorians cited earlier, Arnold (1995) found that the women with the highest aspirations differed from their peers in their expectation that they would have continuous careers. Aspirations for top careers, professionally related experience, and mother's education characterized the females who planned to pursue the most challenging careers. The women with higher career aspirations also planned more continuous labor force participation, as well as later marriage and childbearing than their female peers. At the age of 31, three quarters of the women who had held the highest aspirations were found to be working at the highest levels. This group included physicians, attorneys, professors, scientists, and business executives. Another group included women in middle-ranked occupations such as nursing, physical therapy, and precollege teaching. The third group of women were working in nonprofessional jobs that did not require a college degree or raising their children full-time.

Many women take time off from their careers during their mid-20s to mid-30s to raise children, which is, unfortunately, precisely the time when most careers escalate. It is possible, in some careers, to take time away to raise a family. It is impossible in other careers, however, and this reality results in one of the most difficult decisions facing women. The 10 years between ages 25 and 35 have also been found to be the strongest predictor of lifetime earnings. Our society needs new models that identify ways that women can work, have families, and still be successful. Job sharing, reduced hours, work at home, flexible scheduling, and a variety of creative solutions all address the dilemmas facing women who struggle with these issues. As more women pursue these various future directions, businesses and institutions should continue to develop new suggestions and strategies for promoting female success.

Self-Doubt, Self-Criticism, and Comparisons

From the earliest ages, girls have been found to lack confidence when compared to boys of the same age. Bardwick (1972) found that girls who were as young as 6–8 lacked confidence and expected to fail when compared to boys of the same age who expected to achieve. *Shortchanging Girls, Shortchanging America*, a study commissioned by the American Association of University Women (AAUW, 1991), included a poll of 3,000 students in grades 4–10 that found that, as girls get older, their self-esteem drops dramatically. Enthusiastic and assertive at ages 8 and 9, they begin to lose confidence in their abilities at ages 13 and 14 and emerge from high school with measurably lowered goals. The same study indicated that the decrease in girls' self-esteem is three times greater than boys.

Arnold's (1995) study showed that, as female valedictorians got older, they lowered their self-rankings and seemed to have more doubts about their own abilities, despite receiving higher grades throughout college. She cited Meredith, a Phi Beta Kappa graduate in mathematics and music, as being deeply insecure about applying to graduate school: "I thought no one wanted me" (p. 107). Reis (1998) found insecurities in talented females parallel at almost every age level, as they express more doubt about their abilities, compare themselves more, and criticize themselves and others more. Unfortunately, this critical nature often extends to withholding support from other women.

Even the most talented women worry about criticism and sometimes doubt their ability and work. Physicist Maria Goeppert Mayer had to be pushed to publish her work because she was reluctant to present a detailed account of her ideas to the scientific community at large, fearing that her ideas were not original (Gabor, 1995). She published a brief explanatory letter about her findings in *Physical Review* and only later submitted lengthy articles about her discovery of the shell model, for which she later won the Nobel Prize.

Several different researchers have found that a lack of confidence in girls seems to increase with females who are more intelligent, and this pattern may continue into mid-life. The roots of the problem are deep and complex. Charmaine Gilbreath, a rocket scientist at the Naval Research Laboratory in Washington, DC, heads the electro-optics technology section. Her work involves shooting laser beams at rocket plumes to study reflected light and learn how particles in rocket fuel react with the atmosphere. After completing her first college degree in communications and humanities and deciding to become a lawyer, she changed her plans, deciding she liked physics and geometry. She recalled:

> It took me two years to get up the nerve to take a pre-calculus class. I was surprised that it wasn't that hard. I aced it. Then I took physics and calculus courses, and they weren't all that hard either. That's when I first realized I'd been buffaloed. (Cole, 1994, pp. 58–59)

When she returned to school to get her degree in physics and engineering, she found her biggest obstacle was her own lack of self-confidence: "Girls think they have to always get A's. If a girl gets a B or C, she thinks she can't do it. But boys get B's and C's and go on to be scientists and engineers" (Cole, 1994, pp. 58–59). Explaining the success of some of the current crop of female scientists, Gilbreath, who completed her Ph.D. at Johns Hopkins, explained:

> I had to put psychological blinders on, and not listen to the external stuff, because before, the external stuff had been wrong for me. Those of us who made it are those who learned to ignore society's traditional expectations of women. (Cole, 1994, p. 59)

Numerous studies have documented the difference in self-confidence between men and women relative to achievement (Erkut, 1983; Gold, Brush, & Sprotzer, 1980; Vollmer, 1986). In addition to having less confidence in their own abilities, talented girls are overly critical of themselves and listen more to advice given by others, take it more to heart, and often follow it.

Roberts (1991) found that women look to others for evidence of their competence more than men do and are more sensitive to the evaluations they receive from others (Roberts & Nolen-Hoeksema, 1994). Research has also found that women take criticism much more seriously. Roberts and Nolen-Hoeksema believe that women are more influenced by the evaluations they receive than men, perhaps because of differing perceptions of the informative value of those evaluations. If a guidance counselor tells a young girl that an advanced math class will be too hard, she may not take the math class. If parents tell their daughter that medical school is beyond her capabilities, she may believe them.

Miller (1976) found that the women she saw in her practice were preoccupied with how their actions affected others, questions about connecting and giving, and whether they were perceived as being selfish or measuring up. Her female patients ranged from those who were angry that they did not have the time to pursue their dreams, to those who reached their goals, but were lacking in personal connections and relationships and believed that they were missing something essential in their lives.

Many gifted females also wonder aloud if their success has been gained through compromising what they have done for others (Reis, 1998). Why do so many women feel guilty, selfish, or both about pursuing their own talents? Why, even when they have been successful, are they plagued with guilt and concerns about the impact of their success on those they love? Perhaps the answer lies in what they have been taught as children, or perhaps it lies in what seems to be fundamentally important to women: the relationships. This may explain the happiness of the many women who have given up some of their career dreams or professional aspirations and instead created a happy and fulfilling personal life, rich in relations. Again, however, the paradox emerges as many gifted females look back with deep regret on dreams left unfulfilled. These women often have a sense of destiny and a need to find appropriate work to feel that their lives have somehow made a difference. At the same time, they also seem to realize that work without relationships leaves a woman unhappy in her personal life.

Religious Training

Men are superior to women . . .
—Qur'an 4:34

Blessed are thou, O Lord our God and King of the Universe, that didst not create me a woman.
—Daily prayer of the orthodox male Jew

To the women he said, I will greatly multiply your pain in childbearing; in pain you shall bring forth children, yet your desire shall be for your husband and he shall rule over you.
—Genesis 3:16

Many talented women who have firm religious backgrounds and beliefs have grappled with the religious training they received as young children (Reis, 1998). This religious training may conflict with what is required if they are to develop their own talents. Selflessness, modesty, turning the other cheek, and the subjugation of individual pursuits for the good of others are lessons some women learn from their earliest interaction with religious training, and these lessons may conflict with experiences that occur later in life.

Concerns about pursuing one's talents being misconstrued as "selfish consideration" have been mentioned repeatedly by many gifted women who had religious training throughout their childhood and adolescence. Many still struggle with learned beliefs that to pursue their own talents is selfish. Guilt seems intertwined with many women's struggles to understand the relationship between their own talent development and what they learned in their religious training about their responsibilities to those they love. The guilt they feel possibly explains why selecting work that results in social change or the improvement of the human condition is so important to some talented women with strong religious backgrounds.

Loneliness Experienced by Gifted Women

In many of the interviews conducted with both older and younger gifted females, they described their feelings of loneliness and betrayal by other women (Reis, 1998). When asked about friendships, a successful college president replied simply, "I have none." Some of the reasons that many talented women have few friends and are often lonely revolve around the extremely limited amount of time they have for friendships and the ambivalence others feel about women who achieve at high levels. Successful women often recount situations in which their success was viewed negatively by both other women and men. Women who have successful careers often report that they were pitted against women who stayed at home and worked to raise their families.

Other women actually look for specific examples of deficiencies in their talented counterparts. "She actually said to me, 'Well, of course you earned a law degree, but your marriage fell apart,'" confided one woman, describing her best friend's comment after her painful divorce from her husband who had been having an extramarital relationship. Many gifted and talented women consciously hide their accomplishments from friends and families and often feel guilty about them. Frequent comments made to talented women by their peers and friends include "I don't know how you do it, I certainly can't," "How do you get so much done?," and "Look at what you have accomplished as compared to what I have accomplished." These remarks seem to imply that there is one secret to being successful, rather than the multitude of factors that contribute to achievement in most gifted women: hours of sacrifice, time spent on work instead of other areas, and choices, often painfully made, about what to give up so that one's work can be completed (Reis, 1998).

Many women need and look for support from females and male peers and instead find comparisons, hostility, and a continued absence of friendship. Some women do not extend support to other women and, in turn, rarely find the support they need for their own individual choices. Talented females need to establish a network of support and encouragement from their parents, siblings, and friends. They need someone to be proud of their efforts and the results of their work. Without this support, they will continue to be lonely and isolated.

Physical Attractiveness

In a recent interview, former Congresswoman Pat Schroeder remembered her frustrations with how difficult it was to find a position as an attorney after graduating from Harvard Law School in 1964. She could not secure a single interview with a Denver law firm. Although the Denver firms were interested in her husband, who also had a law degree, they were not interested in her. She also reported that the Harvard placement office, which at that time took for granted the masculine marketplace, did not help her either. Schroeder remembered the placement officer telling women to look ugly, roll their nylons down around their ankles, and look dowdy because an attractive woman would be a detriment in a law office, but an unattractive woman could be stuck in a back room taking care of research files.

Clearly, times have changed, but some physically attractive gifted females report their most challenging conflicts have been about personal issues and choices (Reis, 1998). Teenage girls who are considered attractive are sought after by young males, increasing the likelihood that they will have more decisions to make about relationships and, perhaps, more options to marry younger. They are also more sought after for friendships by other females. Girls who are considered less attractive may have more time to pursue their own choices and can devote more attention to their academic work without facing some of the difficult issues about relationships. Research with high school and middle school girls has found that other students pressured those who were considered attractive for dates, attention, and relationships with both male and female peers. They had little time for introspection about what is important in life (Reis & Diaz, 1999).

In research with gifted teenage girls, some very attractive young women invented boyfriends to give them an excuse not to date, allowing them more time to pursue their work in school and their own interests. Gifted young women from Puerto Rican or other Latina groups reported that inventing boyfriends enabled them to achieve while being able to exist within their culture, which views relationships as crucial. Rosa, one of the young women in a study of gifted high school girls, did not date at all until her junior year of high school, and then she invented a boyfriend who was away at college. She explained that, as a talented Puerto Rican female, dating meant that she would have to put her hopes and dreams on hold and pay attention to her boyfriend: "It's not that I'm not interested. It's just that I see myself doing my thing first. Males always have to be first in a relationship. And, sometimes, they don't like that you're smart" (Reis, Hébert, Diaz, Maxfield, & Ratley, 1995).

While beauty has long been considered a positive attribute in the psychological literature, Heilman and Stopeck (1985a) found that it can be detrimental for women in the corporate world. In one study using 113 randomly selected men and women, participants were asked to review career descriptions and photographs of fictitious important corporate executives. While attractive male business executives were perceived as having more integrity than unattractive men, attractive females were considered to have less integrity than unattractive ones. Attractive male executives were believed to have ability and effort directly related to their success, while the success of attractive females was attributed directly to luck, not ability. Heilman and Stopeck also found that all unattractive female executives were believed to have more integrity and to be more capable than attractive female executives. In another study (Heilman & Stopeck, 1985b), the same research team found that attractiveness was advantageous for women in nonmanagerial positions and disadvantageous for women in managerial positions. Physical attractiveness had no effect whatsoever on males in the same types of positions.

Confusion About Passivity and Assertiveness and Ambivalence About Ambition and Accommodation

Confusion about how to balance success seems to trouble many talented women with a "feminine" personality. Maria Goeppert Mayer once had a conversation with her son, Peter, in which she was critical of at least one woman whom she considered a "pushy" female scientist at the University of Chicago. She said, "I was like that once . . . so I pulled back and then everything came to me" (Gabor, 1995, p. 142).

Being perceived as pushy, aggressive, or even ambitious is troubling to many talented females who often consciously or unconsciously refrain from speaking too much for many reasons. Fear of sounding too aggressive or too smart, stereotypical views about who should speak more often, manners that have been instilled by parents, and other issues related to negative perceptions from the opposite sex cause smart women to become confused about their roles. This confusion confronts young girls almost from the moment they consciously begin to understand that there is an opposite sex. What kind of person am I? Who do I act like? If I talk too much and am reprimanded at home, why should I speak out in school?

Reis (1998) found in interviews with both young girls and older women that too much attention paid to manners in childhood can cripple a talented girl's attitude and her ability to question and speak out. "Don't interrupt." "Don't ask so many questions." "Don't raise your hand so much." "Don't be so aggressive." These types of admonishments from parent to child plant the first seeds of passivity that may eventually create a young woman who doesn't ask questions, doesn't raise her hand, and gives up speaking out in class.

So What Comes First? My Work or Those I Love?

The greatest conflict for talented women in their 20s, 30s, and 40s concerns the interaction between their career and personal lives. This intensely personal struggle to develop their talents while they also meeting the needs of those they love causes gifted women the most conflict, guilt, and pain. Maric Mileva Einstein, Albert Einstein's first wife, was a gifted, high-potential mathematician and fellow classmate at the prestigious Swiss Federal Polytechnic. In a biographical study of her life, Andrea Gabor (1995) found that "the more insecure Maric became in her relationship with Einstein, the more she came to identify her interests with his, ultimately putting Einstein's welfare ahead of her own" (p. 12). After she married Albert and had their children, her life changed drastically. Friends recalled that she often spent all day cleaning, cooking, and caring for the children and then would busy herself in the evening proofreading her husband's work and doing mathematical calculations to help him in his writings.

Constructing a personal and professional life for gifted women is an intensely difficult challenge, and putting the needs of their husbands or partners ahead of their own is an ongoing personal decision that is not often effectively reconciled in many women's lives. Consider the reflections of Mary Catherine Bateson (1990), the daughter of Margaret Meade: "As a young woman, I never questioned the assumption that when I married what I could do would take second place to what my husband could do" (p. 40).

This cultural dilemma is described by writer Susan Faludi, author of *Backlash* (1992), who believes she is leading the life her mother was denied. When Faludi was growing up, she was torn:

> I would look at the women in my neighborhood, and they were all mothers, Cub Scout leaders and cooking chocolate chip cookies, and part of me wanted to grow up and have a station wagon. But the other part of me wanted to be mayor of New York City. (Pogash, 1992, p. 67)

Doris Kearns Goodwin (1997), a noted historian, had similar feelings, which developed after spending a day at work with her father, a bank executive:

> Before this day, I had felt that my father and the other men had moved in a world of interests inaccessible to me; now I had glimpsed the other side, and I resolved someday to enter that larger world. I would go to work like my father, and yet I would somehow keep house the way my mother did, preparing lunch when the kids came home from school. How I would accomplish this I did not know, but the desire stayed with me. (p. 105)

Most women assume the responsibilities for childcare, after-school care, summer activities, camps, homework, and other related child issues. Sandra Day O'Connor became the first woman to serve as the majority leader of a state senate. What is described as an extremely hectic work life by biographer Andrea Gabor (1995), though, never interfered with her family life. "Come 4:30 or 4:45, she would collect her handbag and say in that matter-of-fact way of hers: 'I have to go home now and get dinner ready" (p. 261). Day O'Connor made accommodations, however, including having full-time household help, hiring teenagers to drive her children to their sports practices, and finding other types of support, which allowed her to keep a schedule that even her sons found exhausting. She went to PTA meetings, checked homework, and typed all of her children's papers until they took typing classes at school. Surviving on limited sleep, she worried about her sons and seems to have paid attention to every detail of their childhood while simultaneously trying to let them develop their own independence.

In addition to the responsibilities of children, more recent years have seen an added wrinkle to the complex decisions facing women. Just when many enter the time in which their responsibilities to their children decrease, they struggle to cope with the responsibilities of taking care of aging parents. A different pattern has emerged for women and men regarding care of elderly parents: While sons typically offer financial assistance, daughters and daughters-in-law more often provide the hands-on care.

Conclusion

The accomplishments of some gifted females and the underachievement of others is a complex issue dependent upon many factors, including personal choices and decisions. Our current societal structure virtually eliminates the possibility that the majority of gifted females who marry and have children can achieve at a similar level as their male counterparts, at least for the minimum 18-year commitment they make to raising a child. While the importance of maternal or family giftedness to our society cannot be underestimated, it is often not enough for women who want more or for women who have a sense of destiny about making a difference in the world. While our society has a critical need for those who excel in traditional female careers, such as teaching and nursing, decisions to pursue these careers should be considered by those who have been exposed to a full range of options.

Gifted young females should explore careers and further education and plan and pursue professional opportunities that will challenge their intellect, as well as fit into their personal plans for the future. Families, schools, and businesses need to offer talented women across the lifespan opportunities that will enable them to examine and pursue their personal choices. Talented women should learn to assess and determine whether they are finding the time needed for their own talent development. If they are not able to develop their talents, they should learn to examine why and be proactive about what is required to help them to realize their potential.

The exploration and discussion of the personality issues and personal choices facing talented girls and women should be encouraged. Personality development is intricate and complex. What one young girl regards as an impossible obstacle may be regarded as an intriguing challenge by another. Resilience, rebellion, multipotentiality, different cycles of creativity, and extremely high achievement in the face of obstacles, such as poverty and a complete absence of support, characterize the lives of many gifted women. Yet, they persist. Can this type of persistence, determination, and will be learned, or is it the result of innate personality traits? Many gifted women developed these characteristics throughout their lives, and it is precisely this act of development that creates their success—an active, evolutionary success learned throughout their lifespan. Exploring how and when they develop these characteristics will help all of us to guide gifted females in their journeys at all stages in their lives.

References

American Association of University Women (AAUW). (1991). *Shortchanging girls, shortchanging America: A call to action.* Washington, DC: Author.

Arnold, K. (1995). *Lives of promise.* San Francisco: Jossey-Bass.

Bandura, A. (1986). *Social foundations of thought and action: A social cognitive theory.* Englewood Cliffs, NJ: Prentice Hall.

Bardwick, J. M. (Ed.). (1972). *Readings on the psychology of women.* New York: Harper & Row.

Bateson, M. C. (1990). *Composing a life.* New York: Plume.

Buescher, T. M., Olszewski, P., & Higham, S. J. (1987). *Influences on strategies adolescents use to copy with their own recognized talents.* (Report No. EC 200 755). Paper presented at the biennial meeting of the Society for Research in Child Development, Baltimore, MD.

Clance, P. R. (1985). The imposter phenomenon. *New Woman, 15*(7), 40–43.

Clance, P. R., & Imes, S. (1978). The imposter phenomenon in high achieving women: Dynamics and therapeutic intervention. *Psychotherapy: Theory, research, and practice, 15,* 241–245.

Clark, B. (1992). *Growing up gifted: Developing the potential of children at home and at school* (4th ed.). New York: Merrill.

Cole, K. C. (1994, March). Science discovers women. *Lears,* 56–61, 82–83.

Dabrowski, K. (1967). *Personality-shaping through positive disintegration.* Boston: Little, Brown.

Debold, E., Wilson, M., & Malave, I. (1993). *Mother daughter revolution: From good girls to great women.* Redding, MA: Addison-Wesley.

Dweck, C. S. (1986). Motivation processes affecting learning. *American Psychologist, 41,* 1040–1048.

Ehrlich, V. (1982). *Gifted children: A guide for parents and teachers.* Englewood Cliffs, NJ: Prentice Hall.

Erkut, S. (1983). Exploring sex differences in expectancy, attribution, and academic achievement. *Sex Roles, 9,* 217–231.

Faludi, S. (1992). *Backlash: The undeclared war against American women.* New York: Anchor Books.

Fennema, E., Peterson, P. L., Carpenter, T. P., & Lubinski, C. A. (1990). Teachers' attributions and beliefs about girls, boys, and mathematics. *Educational Studies in Mathematics, 21,* 55–69.

Fredrickson, R. H. (1979). Preparing gifted and talented students for the world of work. *Journal of Counseling and Development, 64,* 556–557.

Fredrickson, R. H. (1986). The multipotential as vocational decision-makers. In R. H. Fredrickson & J. W. M. Rothney (Eds.), *Recognizing and assisting multipotential youth.* Columbus, OH: Merrill.

Gabor, A. (1995). *Einstein's wife: Work and marriage in the lives of five great twenty-first century women.* New York: Viking/Penguin.

Gilligan, C. (1982). *In a different voice: Psychological theory and women's development.* Cambridge, MA: Harvard University Press.

Gilman, C. P. (1898). *Women and economics: A study of the economic relation between men and women as a factor in social evolution.* Boston: Small, Maynard.

Gold, A. R., Brush, L. R., & Sprotzer, E. R. (1980). Developmental changes in self-perceptions of intelligence and self-confidence. *Psychology of Women Quarterly, 5,* 670–680.

Goodwin, D. K. (1997). *Wait till next year: A memoir.* New York: Simon & Schuster.

Hamachek, D. E. (1978). Psycho-dynamics of normal and neurotic perfectionism. *Psychology, 15,* 27–33.

Heilman, M. E., & Stopeck, M. H. (1985a). Being attractive, advantage or disadvantage? Performance-based evaluations and recommended personnel actions as a function of appearance, sex, and job type. *Organizational Behavior and Human Decision Processes, 35,* 202–215.

Heilman, M. E., & Stopeck, M. H. (1985b). Attractiveness and corporate success: Different causal attributions for males and females. *Journal of Applied Psychology, 70,* 379–388.

Holland, D. C., & Eisenhart, M. A. (1990). *Educated in romance: Women, achievement, and college culture.* Chicago: University of Chicago Press.

Hollinger, C. L., & Fleming, E. S. (1984). Internal barriers to the realization of potential correlates and interrelationships among gifted and talented female adolescents. *Gifted Child Quarterly, 28,* 135–139.

Horner, M. S. (1970). Femininity and successful achievement: A basic inconsistency. In J. Bardwick (Ed.), *Feminine personality and conflict* (pp. 45–76). Belmont, CA: Brooks/Cole.

Jepsen, D. A. (1979). Helping gifted adolescents with career exploration. In N. Colangelo & R. T. Zaffrann (Eds.), *New voices in counseling the gifted* (pp. 277–283). Dubuque, IA: Kendall/Hunt.

Kerr, B. A. (1981). Career education strategies for the gifted. *Journal of Career Education, 7,* 318–324.

Kirschenbaum, R. J., & Reis, S. M. (1997). Conflicts in creativity: Talented female artists. *Creativity Research Journal, 10,* pp. 251–263.

Ludwig, M. M. (1996, July/August). Women in the Olympics: A sport psychology perspective. *Coaching Women's Basketball,* 30–32.

Marshall, B. C. (1981). A career decision making pattern of gifted and talented adolescents: Implications for career education. *Journal of Career Education, 7,* 305–310.

Meece, J. L., Blumenfeld, P. C., & Hoyle, R. H. (1988). Students' goal orientations and cognitive engagement in classroom activities. *Journal of Educational Psychology, 80,* 514–523.

Miller, J. B. (1976). *Toward a new psychology of women.* Boston: Beacon Press.

Perrone, P. A., & Van Den Heuvel, D. (1981). Career development of the gifted. *Journal of Career Education, 7,* 299–304.

Pintrich, P. R., & Blumenfeld, P. C. (1985). Classroom experience and children's self-perceptions of ability, effort, and conduct. *Journal of Educational Psychology, 77,* 646–657.

Pogash, C. (1992, April). The brains behind *Backlash*. *Working Women, 17,* 64–68.

Reis, S. M. (1995). Older women's reflections on eminence: Obstacles and opportunities. *Roeper Review, 18,* 66–72.

Reis, S. M. (1998). *Work left undone: Compromises and challenges of talented females.* Mansfield Center, CT: Creative Learning Press.

Reis, S. M., & Diaz, E. (1999). Economically disadvantaged urban female students who achieve in schools. *The Urban Review 31*(1), 31–54.

Reis, S. M., Hébert, T. P., Diaz, E. I., Maxfield, L. R., & Ratley, M. E. (1995). *Case studies of talented students who achieve and under-achieve in an urban high school.* (Research Report 95120). Storrs: National Research Center on the Gifted and Talented, University of Connecticut.

Roberts, T. A. (1991). Gender and the influence of evaluations on self-assessments in achievement settings. *Psychological Bulletin, 109,* 297–308.

Roberts, T. A., & Nolen-Hoeksema, S. (1994). Gender comparisons in responsiveness to others' evaluations in achievement settings. *Psychology of Women Quarterly, 18,* 221–240.

Rutter, M. (1987). Psychological resilience and protective mechanisms. *American Journal of Orthopsychiatry, 37,* 317–331.

Sanborn, M. P. (1979). Career development: Problems of gifted and talented students. In N. Colangelo & R. T. Zaffran (Eds.), *New voices in counseling the gifted* (pp. 284–300). Dubuque, IA: Kendall/Hunt.

Sassen, G. (1980). Success anxiety in women: A constructivist interpretation of its source and its significance. *Harvard Education Review, 50*(1), 13–24.

Schroer, A. C. P., & Dorn, F. J. (1986). Enhancing the career and personal development of gifted college students. *Journal of Counseling and Development, 64,* 567–571.

Schmitz, C. C., & Galbraith, J. (1985). *Managing the social and emotional needs of the gifted: A teacher's survival guide.* Minneapolis, MN: Free Spirit.

Schuler, P. A. (1997). *Characteristics and perceptions of perfectionism in gifted adolescents in a rural school environment.* Unpublished doctoral dissertation, University of Connecticut, Storrs.

Schunk, D. H. (1984). Sequential attributional feedback and children's achievement behaviors. *Journal of Educational Psychology, 75,* 511–518.

Siegle, D., & Reis, S. M. (1998). Gender differences in teacher and student perceptions of students' ability and effort. *Gifted Child Quarterly, 42,* 39–47.

Silverman, L. K. (Ed.). (1993). *Counseling the gifted and talented.* Denver: Love.

Sternberg, R. J., & Lubart, T. I. (1995). *Defying the crowd: Cultivating creativity in a culture of conformity.* New York: The Free Press.

Vollmer, F. (1986). Why do men have higher expectancy than women? *Sex Roles, 14,* 351–362.

Walker, B. A., Reis, S. M., & Leonard, J. S. (1992). A developmental investigation of the lives of gifted women. *Gifted Child Quarterly, 36,* 201–206.

Weiner, B. (1986). *An attributional theory of motivation and emotion.* New York: Springer-Verlag.

Werner, E. E. (1984). Research in review: Resilient children. *Young Children, 40,* 68–72.

Woolf, V. (1957). *A room of one's own.* New York: Harcourt, Brace & Jovanovich.

section two

Social/
Emotional
and
Classroom
Strategies

chapter 4

Recognizing and Meeting the Special Needs of Gifted Females

by Leigh A. Rolnicki

ervasive loss of resilience in talented young women is a tragedy that continues to affect our nation. While about half of the nation's gifted and talented children consists of females, they are conspicuously absent from leadership positions in the adult world (Fox & Tobin, 1988). Based upon our knowledge of young school-aged girls and boys, this fact is quite shocking. Because of their demonstrated potential and career aspirations verbalized at a young age, gifted girls are expected to perform well throughout their educational and professional lives. In contrast to this expectation, researchers have reported that gifted female students still face inequities, are still not achieving at the expected levels, and are not choosing career options commensurate with their cognitive abilities (Callahan, Cunningham, & Plucker, 1994; Lewis, Karnes, & Knight, 1995).

The results of this underachievement go far beyond the loss to society. Many gifted women look back over their lives and perceive numerous missed opportunities (Sears & Barbee, 1977; White, 1984). This loss is not only societal, but very personal in terms of life satisfaction. To facilitate a safer journey through adolescence and to increase the likelihood of a self-determined future, educators must understand the complexity of gifted females and their psychological development.

The Gifted Female in the Classroom

Childhood

Gifted girls begin their school careers feeling highly competent (Silverman, 1994/1995). This feeling of self-confidence is exhibited on playing fields, in classrooms, and in social situations. Hancock (1989) described gifted girls aged 7–10:

> Heady with the power that comes from genuine competence, she brims with initiative. The faster she can run, the higher she can jump, the more she is admired. Being a girl is secondary to being an athlete, a wizard at word games . . . Sharp shooter and ballet dancer, spelling champion and botanist, applauded for being both smart and strong, she is mistress of excellence. (p. 8)

At this age, gifted girls seem eternally resilient. Their energy is inspirational and exhausting to the awestruck observer. Their positive self-concept and internal locus of control are instrumental as they focus on "being." These qualities allow gifted girls in childhood extensive latitude in taking risks, which allows them to explore with greater depth themselves and their surrounding world.

Gifted girls in childhood are not only satisfied, but stimulated by their giftedness. Studies by Loeb and Jay (1987) regarding self-concept in gifted youth report that gifted females in grades 4–6 perceive their giftedness as an asset. Their abilities in the classroom are evidence to them of their certain futures as doctors, lawyers, and scientists. Further research by Li (1988) has shown gifted females to have a more positive perception of their scholastic abilities than gifted males or nongifted females of the same age. At this stage of development, the acknowledgment and acceptance of gifts in academia propel gifted girls in childhood to the top of the class.

Adolescence

As adolescence approaches, culture redefines the priorities of gifted girls. The ominous cloud of a shaping culture hovers above them with "pruning shears, ruthlessly trimming back their spirit" (Hancock, 1989, p.18). These once resilient, confident girls are thrust into a world of confusion. Where merely "being" was once natural and encouraged, "pleasing" is now what is expected. Here they start the molding process of what they think others want them to become, and they subsequently lose sight of what they wanted to become. Caught in a bind between their intelligence and their gender, gifted females in adolescence no longer function with the free spirit that once fueled them in childhood (Hollinger, 1983; Rodenstein, Pfleger, & Colangelo, 1977; Schwartz, 1980).

Research has documented that peers of both sexes tend to reject girls who appear to be too smart (Noble, 1989). Gifted girls, possessing heightened awareness and sensitivity, perceive this rejection and make changes to eradicate the feelings of exclusion. In doing so, they hide their abilities and accomplishments in an effort to conform to the standards established by society (Buescher, Olszewski, & Higham, 1987; Higham & Navarre, 1984; Kramer, 1991). Now valued for appearances, rather than abilities, gifted girls often abandon their aspirations as they learn to adapt to traditional feminine roles (Wells, 1985). Once encouraged to become doctors, they are now guided to become nurses. An early love and commitment to the outdoors that once brought encouragement to become environmental engineers, in adolescence brings instead encouragement to channel those interests into becoming science teachers. Each of these latter occupations undoubtedly has value. Yet, it is critical to note that working in these occupations is not what the young gifted girl sought to achieve.

College/Adulthood

Chickering (1969) suggested that only when females have developed a secure sense of self can they develop appropriate career aspirations and base career decisions on deeply held values. Still reeling from the tumultuous journey through adolescence, gifted females at the college level have likely not possessed a secure sense of self for perhaps 10 years. The values these gifted females currently hold are often not their own, but those dictated by society. Critical, lifelong decisions regarding career and family are often made with little assistance, little foresight, and even less confidence.

At best, gifted females' college experiences have been described as discouraging with regard to career and educational aspirations (Hall & Sandler, 1982). Confusion is a hallmark for females of this age as they move into the adult world, wondering how to merge career, marriage, and family with little or no guidance regarding future planning strategies. Kerr (1988) suggested that gifted females are unsure of how to manage both areas of their lives; thus, many gifted females make choices they later regret. Silverman (1994/1995) viewed this dilemma as a "Sophie's Choice":

> If she chooses to be true to herself, to honor her drive for achievement and self-actualization, she breaks some unspoken rule and faces disconnection, taunts, and rejection from both male and female peers. If she chooses to give up her dreams, to hold herself back, to redirect her energies into the feminine spheres . . . she is accepted and rewarded for her efforts. (p. 146)

Cultural expectations demand that "females should be selfless, nurturing, giving, passive, dependent, and feminine" (Rodenstein et al., 1977, p. 120). These expectations, coupled with multipotentiality in achievement, create conflicts nearly impossible for the gifted female to resolve.

Development of Self-Esteem in Females

A common thread running through the aforementioned stages of development is self-esteem. The importance of self-esteem in relation to achievement and general life satisfaction is paramount. Understanding the distinctive differences in the development of self-esteem in females is critical to solving this dilemma. More specifically, acknowledging and understanding the shift in self-esteem between childhood and adolescence and then on into adulthood may be the critical first step in affecting change for this population.

Self-esteem, as defined in the *American Heritage Dictionary*, is "satisfaction with oneself" (p. 619). While this definition is written to be universal and gender nonspecific, the paths taken by males and females in the development of self-esteem are far different. Yahne and Long (1988) reported four distinct themes regarding female's development of self-esteem: (a) females develop differently from males within a context of relationships; (b) maturing is often facilitated by the collapse of cherished assumptions; (c) forging self-concepts that are both positive and feminine is difficult; and (d) females are challenged to include themselves as objects of their own care, choice, and responsibility.

The first theme, constructed by Chodorow (1978) and supported by Gilligan (1982), concluded that females come to know themselves as they are known through their relationships with others. That is, as females go through life, their identities rest not upon who they are as individuals, but who they are to others. Depending upon others to define who they are and to what degree they are intelligent, females reduce their own awareness of themselves. As a result, future plans are made without regard to deeply held values of the female, and instead they are made based upon external beliefs. The result could be dips in self-esteem over time, especially when the relationships are threatened.

The second theme—the collapse of cherished assumptions initiating change—was consistently supported in various studies (Yahne & Long, 1988). Unpredictable critical events forced females to rethink their values and life direction (Sangiuliano, 1980). In previous male-driven studies related to the development of self-esteem, predictable, age-related, or developmental events were noted as precursors to change. For females, however, the unpredictable events were those that led to a realignment of values and the forced impetus to change life direction. Again, an outside force created the change or movement, rather than the inner choice or drive to change.

In the third theme, researchers found that females face great difficulty in the quest to integrate womanhood and adulthood. Studies have found that positive and feminine self-concepts are incongruent (Yahne & Long, 1988). According to Hayes (1986), as females seek to assert themselves by responding to their inner voices, many are concerned that assertive behavior will be interpreted as bitchy, unfeminine, or, even worse, uncaring. This theme is illustrated with clarity beginning in adolescence and is often present throughout much of adulthood.

The fourth and final theme emerging from studies of self-esteem development and females is the challenge they face in including themselves as objects of their own care, choice, and responsibility. Females do not hesitate to think of the welfare of others in making life decisions, but more often than not, they neglect themselves and their needs when making critical decisions. Once cognizant of this oversight, the question then becomes: "[I]s it better to respond to others and abandon myself or to respond to myself and abandon others?" (Gilligan, Lyons, & Hanmer, 1990, p. 9). Faced with severed connections that, paradoxically, are the essence of female strength, gifted young women often choose to abandon themselves.

The School: A Shaping Force in the Development of Females

Reduced self-esteem, loss of voice, and failure to realize potential are not the results of a deliberate choice, but of a life-long history of small compromises and adjustments (Kerr, 1988) that are made due to attitudes shaped predominantly by three institutions: home, school, and media (Fox & Tobin, 1988). Through verbal and nonverbal messages, these institutions begin molding gifted girls at a very young age and continue influencing them throughout adulthood. While loss of resilience is pinpointed at adolescence, messages and attitudes igniting this change begin earlier. In an attempt to bring clarity and potential solutions to this problem, this chapter focuses on one of the three shaping cultures: the educational institution.

A concerted effort has been made on the part of parents, teachers, and researchers to eradicate gender bias exhibited in many classrooms in the United States. While teacher behaviors have been analyzed and strategies for reducing the bias have been presented, efforts have brought little change. Perhaps this is due to the fact that the behavior per se is not the problem; it is only a manifestation. Instead, the true problem lies in the deeply rooted belief systems of the teachers who exercise bias. As human beings, teachers are often unaware of attitudes and biases they may possess with regard to gender roles. The values they place on male and female behavior perpetuate the bias they are seeking to end. For instance, an eager, questioning mind often causes bright students to call out in class, debate, argue, or ask questions. Reis (1987) noted that an eager young boy is labeled "precocious," while an eager bright girl is labeled "obnoxious."

Similarly, Welsh (cited in Wells, 1985) found that teachers gave low ratings to girls who were analytical and unconventional in their approaches to solving problems, while males exhibiting the same behaviors were praised. This is because traditional, appropriate behaviors for girls have been passivity and acceptance. Praising these behaviors in the classroom can discourage a lifetime of achievement (Wells), thus educators must be open to a value system that accommodates and encourages choices and intellectual excellence from gifted females, even if this requires a restructuring of themselves.

Saving a Population at Risk Through Intervention

Teachers

During the school years, teachers spend nearly as much time with children as do their parents. This fact increases the importance of positive classroom experiences for all children. Teachers of gifted females should be thoroughly educated about ways to meet their unique academic and affective needs. Because many districts are unsupportive of gifted programs, this awareness requires much self-education on the part of teachers. Teachers should examine their views with regard to gender issues and adjust their teaching styles to enhance the healthy development of all students in the classroom. Creative, analytical problem solvers are what society needs. Boys and girls should be praised for these higher level thought processes that demand critical, reflective thinking. Teachers must adjust their mindsets to encourage thinking behaviors, rather than social behaviors, in females. This will start this major restructuring necessary in U.S. classrooms.

Counselors

School counselors play a pivotal role in guiding gifted girls to achievement and healthy living. Two goals are critical in the development of specialized programming for this population: connection and exploration. To reach these goals, counselors must facilitate homogeneously based support and career development groups to encourage personal and intellectual growth.

Support groups. Females need to share with each other in an environment that encourages self-acceptance and exploration that nurtures their inner voices. Single-sex support groups facilitated from a feminist approach provide opportunities for females to increase their self-esteem by dealing directly and interactively with issues. Additionally, the universality of concerns, fears, and the affirming group experience is a potent motivator for stress reduction and change (Hayes, 1986). The peer interaction resulting from group counseling with females has afforded important advantages for females' psychological health (Hayes; Yahne & Long, 1988). Hayes further noted that

> the effect of actually hearing first-hand other women's struggles to stay afloat in a sea of societal and self-generated expectations cannot be underestimated. The emergence of this universal dilemma motivates members to work on personal agendas. (p. 439)

In the environment of sharing and problem solving, females are better able to identify specific behaviors that contribute to their issues (Hayes, 1986). These same-sex groups can provide a nonthreatening format for clients to begin developing regard for and acceptance of themselves (Fox & Tobin, 1988; Silverman, 1994/1995; Yahne & Long, 1988). The foundational elements emphasized through a person-centered, feminist approach—freedom, choice, values, personal responsibility, autonomy, purpose, and meaning—celebrate uniqueness and give life to the soul (Corey, 1996).

Career development groups. Research indicates that career education classes restricted to females provide more peer interaction than that of mixed-sex classes (Fox & Tobin, 1988; Hay & Bakken, 1991; Silverman, 1991; Wells, 1985). Resulting from this greater sense of cohesiveness, Fox and Tobin believe these homogeneously grouped girls might ultimately choose more nontraditional careers. Therefore, maintaining same-sex grouping for career development groups has a greater impact on this population.

Fox and Tobin (1988) suggested four key goals in their recommendations for specialized career guidance programming for gifted females: (a) introduction to occupational areas relevant to talents; (b) interaction with females in careers being studied; (c) integration of career guidance into the total curriculum; and (d) simulation of work experiences. In essence, Fox and Tobin have sought to implement a meaningful, integrated guidance curriculum that provides exposure to relevant occupations, allows for mentorship-type relationships, and expands opportunities in hands-on learning related to areas of interest.

Kerr (1988) recommended three different levels of sophisticated intervention stressing values as related to career choices. While agreeing with the exposure element found in the Fox and Tobin (1988) model, Kerr suggested that career exposure at the initial stage (Level I) should instead be wide-ranging and indiscriminate in relation to gifted girls' interests, needs, and values. At Level II, gifted girls are encouraged to raise their aspirations within occupations congruent with their vocational personalities. Once they reach Level III, gifted girls are at the value-based career counseling intervention. This involves a group life-planning workshop, an assessment session, and an individual counseling session.

Most distinctive about the Kerr (1988) model in contrast to the Fox and Tobin (1988) model is the heavy emphasis placed on the values clarification of these talented girls. For Kerr, the focus becomes

> the search for meaning rather than the search for a job. Having a sense of purpose may also serve to inoculate gifted females against the compromises and minor defeats which prevent the realization of their potential. (p. 267)

The research indicates that, while each of these models seeks to provide exposure and opportunities for gifted girls, the Kerr model, with its value-based approach, places greater value on the exploration and actualization of the core self.

Overall, career awareness programs for gifted females should expand career interests beyond those professions traditionally considered suitable for females (Fox & Tobin, 1988; Kerr, 1988; Wells, 1985). Expanding overall knowledge of less-well-known careers, along with introducing skills and education needed for these professions, supplies gifted girls with a broader base from which to make career decisions. In creating exposure to potential careers, programs where students perform real tasks of the profession and solve real problems associated with particular careers are found to be most effective and should be an integral part of the career guidance curriculum (Fox & Tobin; Silverman, 1991).

Future research focused on combining the elements of the comprehensive-based model by Fox and Tobin (1988) with the value-based model by Kerr (1988) may lead to even greater results in increasing the number of gifted girls who truly know themselves, realize career potentials, and, in effect, enjoy greater life satisfaction.

Conclusion

Gifted females need the help of parents, teachers, and counselors to work through the web of adolescence and emerge the confident, risk-taking pioneers they were at 8 years of age. Hancock (1989) believes that females are able to bring out the repressed "girl within" if they revisit their childhood experiences. It is encouraging to know that some females eventually find the 8-year-old lost so long ago. However, it is disturbing to consider that approximately 20 to 30 years of gifted women's lives are spent searching for the self that was once whole.

References

Buescher, T. M., Olszewski, P., & Higham, S. J. (1987, April). *Influences on strategies adolescents use to cope with their own recognized talents.* Paper presented at biennial meeting of the Society for Research on Child Development, Baltimore, MA.

Callahan, C., Cunningham, C., & Plucker, J. (1994). Foundations for the future: The socio-emotional development of gifted, adolescent females. *Roeper Review, 17,* 99–104.

Chickering, A. W. (1969). *Education and identity.* San Francisco: Jossey Bass.

Chodorow, N. (1978). *The reproduction of mothering: Psychoanalysis and the sociology of gender.* Berkeley: University of California Press.

Corey, G. (1996). *Theory and practice of counseling and psychotherapy* (4th ed.). Pacific Grove, CA: Brooks Cole.

Fox, L., & Tobin, D. (1988). Broadening career horizons for gifted girls. *Gifted Child Today, 11*(1), 9–13.

Gilligan, C. (1982). *In a different voice: Psychological theory and women's development.* Cambridge, MA: Harvard University Press.

Gilligan, C., Lyons, N., & Hanmer, C. (1990). *Making connections: The relational world of adolescent girls at Emma Willard School.* Cambridge, MA: Harvard University Press.

Hall, R. M., & Sandler, B. R. (1982). *The classroom climate: A chilly one for women?* Washington, DC: Association of American Colleges.

Hancock, E. (1989). *The girl within.* New York: Ballantine Books.

Hay, C., & Bakken, L. (1991). Gifted sixth-grade girls: Similarities and differences in attitudes among gifted girls, non-gifted peers, and their mothers. *Roeper Review, 13,* 158–160.

Hayes, L. (1986). The superwoman myth: Social casework. *The Journal of Contemporary Social Work, 67,* 436–441.

Higham, S. J., & Navarre, J. (1984). Gifted adolescent females require different treatment. *Journal for the Education of the Gifted, 8,* 43–58.

Hollinger, C. (1983). Counseling the gifted and talented female adolescent: The relationship between social self-esteem and traits of instrumentality and expressiveness. *Gifted Child Quarterly, 27,* 157–160.

Kerr, B. (1988). Career counseling for gifted girls and women. *Journal of Career Development, 14,* 259–267.

Kramer, L. R. (1991). The social construction of ability perception: An ethnographic study of gifted adolescent girls. *Journal of Early Adolescence, 11,* 340–362.

Lewis, J., Karnes, F., & Knight, H. (1995). A study of self-actualization and self-concept in intellectually gifted students. *Psychology in the Schools, 32,* 52–60.

Li, A. K. F. (1988). Self-perception and motivational orientation in gifted children. *Roeper Review, 10,* 175–180.

Loeb, R. C., & Jay, G. (1987). Self-concepts in gifted children: Differential impact in boys and girls. *Gifted Child Quarterly, 31,* 9–13.

Noble, K. D. (1989). Living out the promise of high potential: Perceptions of 100 gifted women. *Advanced Development, 1,* 57–75.

Reis, S. M. (1987). We can't change what we don't recognize: Understanding the special needs of gifted females. *Gifted Child Quarterly, 31,* 83–88.

Rodenstein, J., Pfleger, L. R., & Colangelo, N. (1977). Career development of gifted women. *Gifted Child Quarterly, 21,* 340–347.

Sangiuliano, I. (1980). *In her time.* New York: Morrow.

Schwartz, L. L. (1980). Advocacy for the neglected gifted: Females. *Gifted Child Quarterly, 24,* 113–117.

Sears, P. S., & Barbee, A. H. (1977). Career and life satisfactions among Terman's gifted women. In J. C. Stanley, W. C. George, & C. H. Solano (Eds.), *The gifted and the creative: A fifty-year perspective* (pp. 28–65). Baltimore, MD: Johns Hopkins University Press.

Sheehy, G. (1974). *Passages.* New York: Dutton.

Silverman, L. (1991). Helping gifted girls reach their potential. *Roeper Review, 13,* 122–123.

Silverman, L. (1994/1995). To be gifted or feminine. *Journal of Secondary Gifted Education, 6,* 141–153.

Wells, M. (1985, May/June). Gifted females: An overview for parents, teachers, and counselors. *Gifted Child Today,* 43–46.

White, W. L. (1984). *The perceived effects of an early enrichment experience: A fourth year follow-up study of the Speyer School experiment for gifted students.* Unpublished doctoral dissertation, University of Connecticut, Storrs.

Yahne, C., & Long, V. (1988). The use of support groups to raise self-esteem for women clients. *College Health, 37,* 79–84.

chapter 5

Behind the Mask

*exploring the need for specialized
counseling for gifted females*

by Julianne Jacob Ryan

s children, individuals begin playing dress-up,
exploring and temporarily living in make-believe
worlds. The inner-world created by gifted children
is often more intense and more vivid, often having
been created to make up for what they lack in their
own childhood.

As gifted children grow into adolescence and
adulthood, they often experience the need to create
a different type of make-believe self to inhabit in
the everyday world in order to hide their individuality and uniqueness. They must create a façade, a
mask that hides their giftedness, the true self.
Gifted females, in particular, are at high risk of losing themselves behind a mask of conformity.

Loss of Identity

This hiding of the self can arguably be a form
of self-suicide, effectively killing off the true self and
replacing it with a more socially acceptable self. The
loss of the gifted females' true identity is a process

that usually begins by the time the middle grades are reached, at which time the perception of their giftedness changes. It is no longer socially acceptable to be smart; therefore, girls often begin hiding their intelligence, downplaying their abilities, and conforming more to the standards of their peers. In a study of gifted females in grades 1–12, Kline and Short (1991) found that, as gifted girls grow up, their self-confidence progressively declines and their perfectionist tendencies increase. By this stage in their development, gifted girls caught in this trap are more vulnerable to a variety of mental health issues, including depression, eating disorders, and substance abuse (Frost, Marten, Lahart, & Rosenblate, 1990; Kline & Short; Noble, 1989).

Gilligan (1982) hypothesized that girls, typically around the ages of 11 and 12, are pressured by society to lose their personal, unique, and honest self, become ordinary, and take up traditional female roles. Clark (2002) has affirmed this, as well, noting, "As early as the middle school years, values of intimacy and empathy are preferred over all other agendas for girls, compared with male values of competitiveness and individualism" (pp. 516–517). It is not only success that is to be feared, but being viewed as "different or unfeminine by their peers, especially males" (Highham & Navarre, 1984, cited in Hay & Bakken, 1991).

The Results of Mixed Messages

Gifted girls are at special risk for emotional instability due to the mixed messages they receive from family, peers, teachers, and society. Praised for their accomplishments as children, they are often told to negate these accomplishments as adolescents. As a child, intelligence is valued and nurtured; as adolescence descends, girls are overwhelmingly pressured to value such traits as physical attractiveness, poise, modesty, marriagibility, and femininity above all other accomplishments (Silverman, 1993). By the time they are adolescents, gifted girls are asked to choose between beauty/femininity and achievement (Pipher, 1994; Silverman), which is often no choice at all because society's message is that beauty is what is important in a woman, not intelligence. Noble (1989) noted that society effectively tells gifted females that their accomplishments are of little value and that any work of real significance is accomplished by men.

These attitudes often create serious internal strife and an imbalance in personal perceptions of self-worth. For the female who chooses to accept society's mainstream role for her and hides her intelligence, a loss of self-esteem and a lowered self-image is almost inevitable. As the true self is lost, the gifted individual may experience an increase in poor coping skills, depression, guilt, and learned helplessness (Sands & Howard-Hamilton, 1994).

Although there has been little investigation done on the subject, it is hypothesized that gifted females are at a higher risk for eating disorders than their nongifted peers, both in adolescence and adulthood. Factors contributing to this risk include issues of perfectionism, lowered self-esteem, a need for control, and the loss of identity often associated with the onset of adolescence (Kerr, 1985; Noble, 1989; Silverman, 1993). As Pipher (1994) noted, females in today's society are inundated with stereotypes of the "perfect girl." Television, music videos, advertisements, and teenage magazines all emphasize beauty and sexuality above brains and achievement. Youth magazines are filled with beauty and fashion tips and articles about how to get a boyfriend, keep a boyfriend, or get a date to the prom. Little if any space is given to school, achievement, or interpersonal growth issues. Females are told from a very young age that looks and sex appeal are what count in this world.

Eating disorders have also been theorized as stemming from the "perfect girl" syndrome (Brown & Gilligan, 1993). This theory states that, by the time a girl reaches preadolescence, she has been socialized to be the "perfect" child: one who is pretty, obedient, caring, agrees with others, and, above all, never rocks the boat (Brown & Gilligan). The perfect gifted girl is submissive, which, in many instances, causes the "stuffing" of feelings, ideas, and behaviors as they seek to conform to the popular ideal of femininity. At this time, gifted girls stop viewing themselves through their own personal filter and begin judging themselves through the eyes of those around them. This same loss of self-esteem and perfectionism found in gifted females, associated with increased incidents of eating disorders such as anorexia nervosa and bulimia, has also been linked to higher rates of depression, as well as a suicide attempt rate four to five times higher than that of their male peers (Debold, 1995).

Counseling Strategies

When involved in a therapeutic relationship with a gifted individual, one must be aware of the many different affective traits gifted people possess. Of special importance to mental health issues, there are certain commonalties cited by numerous researchers (Clark, 2002; Dabrowski & Piechowski, 1977; Kerr, 1985):

- an unusual degree of sensitivity to the feelings and expectations of others;
- a sharp wit that is often used as a coping and defense mechanism;
- heightened feelings of self, even at very young ages, often accompanied by a strong sense of being different from the rest of the world;
- high idealism and a passionate sense of justice, of right and wrong;
- higher morality than others their age, often higher than society in general;
- emotional supersensitivity, along with great emotional depth;
- high expectations of self and others, often leading to perfectionism; and
- the need for abstract values and actions to compliment each other.

When discussing the needs of gifted females, it is important that strengths are not forgotten. Nearly every problem set forth above has a flip side that can make it a strength. For example, the emotional makeup of gifted people that may cause them so much pain may also provide them with a strong sense of integrity and personal values. Many of these children survive crises due in large part to their sense of humor and different worldview. They can both laugh at the world and laugh with it. They are often great problem solvers, possessing an avid curiosity, tenacity, and a strong will to be healthy.

Therapy With Gifted Girls

Gifted females, from childhood into adulthood, often feel alienated, misunderstood, and unaccepted by others. In her research on gifted women, Noble (1987) found that, unlike their nongifted peers, gifted girls are often expected to hide who they are and conform to societal expectations that do not come naturally to them. Many gifted girls are taught to be feminine, cute, and submissive, while at the same time being told that they are capable of anything a man is. The simultaneous expectations of being a typical housewife and mother and having a strong career are often at odds with one another. This causes intense stress for gifted women and subsequent ambivalence as to their place in society. As a result, by the time they are adults, the majority of gifted women are likely to settle for much less than their potential suggests they are capable of (Noble, 1987). Therefore, an important first step in the therapy process is for the counselor to assist his or her gifted female client in loving herself and becoming comfortable with who she is, thus allowing her to remove her mask and accept her true self, whether society labels that self acceptable or not.

When working with gifted females, the amount of direction provided by the counselor must be flexible and fluid. Working with this population usually requires less direction than a counselor may be used to. According to Silverman (1993), the most effective counselor is one who listens effectively, shares thoughts, offers ideas, shares personal experiences when appropriate, and provides a safe place for the client. Another vital piece of working effectively with this population is having the necessary knowledge base of the particular issues and their unique effects on the gifted.

Feminist therapy techniques are particularly helpful when working with gifted females. This therapy approach assumes that much of the depression women suffer is not a result of pathology, but rather is a symptom of living in a patriarchal society that consistently devalues their self-worth (Sands & Howard-Hamilton, 1994). Using this technique, the therapist and client address the various issues faced by gifted females, such as the forced choice between femininity and intellectualism. What is stressed is that the main source of depression is not a brain imbalance or a skewed perception of a situation, but rather real conflicts stemming from the social and political pressures and notions of the world (Worell & Remer, 1992, as cited in Sands & Howard-Hamilton). Therapy is often directed at increasing a gifted girl's self-esteem and self-concept through the examination of personal value systems and personal beliefs. These values and beliefs are then challenged, helping them reframe their beliefs in ways that encourage personal growth and self-acceptance.

Whatever counseling technique is used, it is essential that, when looking at gifted girls, we look at them as a whole and consider both their strengths and weaknesses; if we focus only on the deficits and the problems, we are creating victims and denying an individual's personal power. The ability to turn problems into strengths is at the core of counseling the gifted. Ultimately, "the ability to achieve success . . . in their lives will most likely be determined by the decision to rely on their strengths rather than to surrender to the many problems which they will undoubtedly encounter as they mature" (Callahan, Cunningham, & Plucker, 1994, p. 104).

Counseling for the Parents of Gifted Girls

The importance of the availability of counseling for the parents of gifted girls cannot be ignored, just as the parental role in a young girl's life cannot be emphasized enough. The way a parent views his or her daughter has more influence on shaping the child's self-perception than actual achievements do. Girls are especially susceptible to parental attitudes and opinions of them due to the fact that they tend to be more emotional and other-oriented than males (Gilligan, 1982). How others view them is as important, if not more important, than their own perception of themselves.

Parents need counselors who can educate them on how to help their offspring overcome the many sexist barriers their gifted female children will undoubtedly encounter on the road to successful, healthy, and fulfilled development. Gifted girls need a "secure an emotional base . . . [and] warm, nurturing parents who encourage exploration, . . . independent thinking, independent behavior and tolerance for change" (Noble, 1987, p. 373). Silverman (1993) suggested that parents of gifted girls should hold high expectations and actively promote risk-taking.

Other ways parents can promote healthy development in their gifted daughter(s) are

- applauding independence and individuality;
- creating a home environment that fosters open and honest communication;
- openly challenging stereotypes and encouraging girls to pursue "male-dominated" activities;
- applauding effort—even when it results in failure and not success;
- allowing failure;
- taking their daughter's opinions and ideas seriously;
- and teaching play and encourage laughter.

Conclusion

While interventions can help counteract the process, if left alone, many gifted girls will find the façade they effected slowly taking over their personality until all they perceive is this false self. By the time adulthood is reached, they have successfully obliterated their true self. This can cause many problems, including depression, loss of perceived ability, self-doubt, lowered self-worth, and feelings of hopelessness and loss. Of course, the real self has never been truly banished; but, remembering and resurrecting what is under the mask is often an arduous and long journey.

Adolescence is a vulnerable time for all teenagers, and gifted girls are no exception. As a former client once remarked, "Being a teenager is hard enough. Being gifted and female is brutal!" There is a common misconception that special services are not needed for the gifted, which is an assumption that would never be made of the mentally handicapped. Yet, both groups represent extreme deviations from the norm. It is unfortunate that, when most counselors think of the gifted population (if they do at all), they labor under the fallacy that these youths have their worlds under complete control, suffer from few personal traumas, and do not need special attention or counseling.

However, the opposite is true. "Giftedness does not preclude the possibility that adolescents will experience serious emotional trauma" (Kline & Meckstroth, 1985, cited in Strip, Swassing, & Kidder, 1991, p. 124). The numerous frustrations, stresses, and special problems coping with life that gifted females encounter have only recently received much attention and study. It is important for counselors to realize that, although most females encounter some strife growing up, "[gifted girls] can, however, experience emotional problems capable of crippling the human spirit" (Schauer, 1976, cited in Strip et al., p. 124). In order for gifted girls to develop into healthy, fulfilled, intellectualized adults, there are a variety of needs that must be addressed. Of greatest importance, they should be assisted in peeling away the mask and discovering who they are so that they may eventually learn to accept and like that true self.

It is for all of the aforementioned issues and reasons that it is not just important, but critical that specialized counseling services be available for gifted females of all ages, as well as for their families. It is important that counselors be aware of the special needs and strengths of this population. Without an adequate understanding of the gifted female "experience," the proper help cannot be offered. Although all people share certain universal experiences and problems, the perspective and the social, emotional, and guidance needs for gifted females are unique.

It is unfortunate that, at the present time, the mental health system basically ignores the needs of gifted females of all ages. Counselors tend to have little knowledge of this population, their problems, or their needs. Perhaps more than any other group, gifted females are the silent subculture. Their psychological needs are basically unmet, or professionals treat them with little or no knowledge of their true natures. This represents a serious lack in the therapeutic process, and, as Schmitz and Galbraith (1985) noted, professional counseling is without doubt one of the best ways to help gifted individuals learn about themselves and their conflicts with the world.

References

Brown, L. M., & Gilligan, C. (1993). *Meeting at the crossroads: Female's psychology and girls' development*. New York: Ballentine Books.

Callahan, C., Cunningham, C., & Plucker, J. (1994). Foundations for the future: The socio-emotional development of gifted, adolescent women. *Roeper Review, 17,* 99–104.

Clark, B. (2002). *Growing up gifted: Developing the potential of children at home and at school* (6th ed.) Upper Saddle River, NJ: Merrill/ Prentice Hall.

Dabrowski, K., & Piechowski, M. M. (1977). *Theory levels of emotional development* (Vol. 1). Oceanside, NY: Dabor Sciences.

Debold, E. (1995). Helping girls survive the middle grades. *Principal, 74*(3), 22–24.

Frost, R. O., Marten, P. Lahart, C., & Rosenblate, R. (1990). The dimensions of perfectionism. *Cognitive Therapy and Research, 14,* 449–468.

Gilligan, C. (1982). *In a different voice: Psychological development* (Vol. 1), Cambridge, MA: Harvard University Press.

Hay, C., & Bakken, L. (1991). Gifted sixth grade girls: Similarities and differences in attitudes among gifted girls, non-gifted peers, and their mothers. *Roeper Review, 13,* 158–160.

Higham, S. J., & Navarre, J. (1984). Gifted adolescent females require differential treatment. *Journal for the Education of the Gifted, 8,* 43–58.

Kerr, B. (1985). *Smart girls, gifted women.* Columbus: Ohio Psychology Press.

Kline, B. E., & Meckstroth, E. A. (1985). Understanding and encouraging the exceptionally gifted. *Roeper Review, 8,* 24–30.

Kline, B., & Short, E. (1991). Changes in emotional resilience: Gifted adolescent females. *Roeper Review, 13,* 118–120.

Noble, K. (1987). The dilemma of the gifted woman. *Psychology of Women Quarterly, 11,* 367–378.

Noble, K. (1989). Counseling gifted women: Becoming heroes of our own stories. *Journal for the Education of the Gifted, 12,* 131–141.

Pipher, M. (1994). *Reviving Ophelia: Saving the selves of adolescent girls.* New York: Ballentine Books.

Sands, T., & Howard-Hamilton, M. (1994). Understanding depression among gifted adolescent females: Feminist therapy strategies. *Roeper Review, 17,* 192–194.

Schauer, G. H. (1976). Emotional disturbance and giftedness. *Gifted Child Quarterly, 20,* 470–477.

Schmitz, C., & Galbraith, J. (1985). *Managing the social and emotional needs of the gifted.* Minneapolis, MN: Free Spirit.

Silverman, L. (1993). Techniques for preventative counseling. In L. K. Silverman (Ed.), *Counseling the gifted and talented* (pp. 81–106). Denver: Love.

Strip, C., Swassing, R., & Kidder, R. (1991). Female adolescents counseling female adolescents: A first step in emotional crisis intervention. *Roeper Review, 13,* 124–129.

Worell, J., & Remer, P. (1992). *Feminist perspectives in therapy: An empowerment model for women.* New York: Wiley.

chapter 6

Using Biography to Counsel Gifted Young Women

by **Thomas P. Hébert, Linda A. Long,**
and **Kristie L. Speirs Neumeister**

> *[T]hinking that I had been given a second chance in life, I threw myself into books. I read books about troubled women, Helen Keller and Anne Frank. I read about Eleanor Roosevelt. . . .*
>
> *What a difference it makes in your world to go into some other life. It's what I love most. I'm reading always to leave myself, always to leave myself behind. That's what reading is. You get to leave.*
>
> —Oprah Winfrey,
> qtd. in Johnson, 1997, pp. 53, 60

ifted young women face a variety of important social and emotional issues throughout adolescence and passage into adulthood, including those related to gender-role expectations, relationship-oriented problems, achievement and underachievement concerns, and the need for resilience in women's lives. The guided reading of biographies is a useful counseling strategy through which middle and high school educators may assist gifted females in gaining helpful insights to deal with the problems they face and will continue to face throughout their lives, thus helping them maintain their emotional health and develop their talent.

Gender-Role Expectations

As early as the preschool and kindergarten years, females begin to internalize learned sex roles (Reis, 1999). Behavior conforming to these sex roles is reinforced by parents and teachers who consistently reward girls for exhibiting traditional female behavior (Mann, 1994; Sadker & Sadker, 1994). Later on, many young women in middle school learn to fear success and avoid involvement in math and science courses following years of societal stereotyping and sex-role socialization (Callahan & Reis, 1996). Stereotyping delivers powerful messages to intelligent young females about their roles in life, their own importance, and their worth as women (Reis & Callahan, 1989). Reis asserted that, even when a gifted young woman is encouraged to study in a field of her choice, the message she receives as an adult is that her success is measured as a wife and mother, not as a professional. Acceptance of sex-role stereotypes regarding their ability may cause gifted young women to lower their expectations for academic and career achievement.

The literature provides evidence that sex-role stereotyping is reinforced in school environments and that teachers may contribute to it (Sadker & Sadker, 1994). Studies have indicated that masculine characteristics and males are more highly valued than female characteristics and females in classrooms during elementary, secondary, and college years (Callahan & Reis, 1996). Callahan and Reis indicated that educators gave lower ratings to girls who were analytic and unconventional in their approaches to problem solving, whereas males exhibiting the same behavior were praised.

Research has also indicated that gifted females receive mixed messages about their roles in society that serve as gender-related barriers to achievement and self-actualization. Hollinger (1991) reported that, in the midst of establishing their gender identity, gifted females discover that societal stereotypes of what it means to be feminine conflict with expectations of gifted students to achieve great things and occupational stereotypes deemed as "masculine." On one hand, society expects them to maintain the traditional feminine role of being less aggressive and assertive than males (Bakken, Hershey, & Miller, 1990; Sadker & Sadker, 1994). On the other hand, gifted girls face societal expectations that, as women, they will use their intelligence to achieve professional success while also maintaining a positive home and family life. Many gifted females become confused about what is expected from professional roles for gifted individuals and stereotypic feminine roles (Reis, 1999).

Literature also suggests that, although gender-role expectations and perceptions of female achievement vary from culture to culture, sexism is a barrier that all groups of gifted women face (Kitano, 1995). Diaz (1998) found that gifted Puerto Rican females often struggle with traditional patriarchal families that reinforced traditional sex-roles. Ford (1995) noted that young gifted African American women face social barriers and racial discrimination that negatively impacted their self-efficacy. Kitano (1995) noted that young Asian women also face conflicts with parents and traditional family values and are often expected to subordinate their goals to those of their male siblings. Kerr (1994) found that gifted Native American women are often reluctant to exhibit their intellectual abilities or call attention to themselves as individuals due to the communal nature of their culture.

Assuming that gifted women prefer any particular role is problematic. Reis and Callahan (1989) suggested that there is no reason why successful professional, wife, and mother must be mutually exclusive categories. Some gifted women succeed in maintaining feminine qualities and traditional roles of wife and mother while also utilizing traditionally masculine qualities in their careers (Piirto, 1991). Personal attributes such as independence, autonomy, and psychological androgyny characterize most gifted females who succeed in their professional careers. These women have successfully resolved the conflict between expectations for gifted students and those for women, while others continue to struggle with making sense of the contradictory messages and role expectations delivered by society (Rimm, Rimm-Kaufman, & Rimm, 1999; Subotnik & Arnold, 1996).

Relationships

Along with gender-role expectations, another significant influence on gifted females' emotional well-being and talent development lies in their relationships with others. The aspirations of gifted females may be shaped by parental attitudes and values, a need to be accepted by their peers and viewed as desirable by males, and a central feeling of responsibility to care for their loved ones.

Family relationships strongly impact gifted girls' self-esteem and achievement, for they internalize their parents' beliefs and values regarding women's ability to succeed (Callahan & Reis, 1996). Reis (1999) noted that, to be successful, girls need to feel confident challenging conventional ideas, questioning authority, and voicing their concerns and ideas for change; however, these characteristics conflict with many parents' conceptions of what is appropriate behavior for a well-mannered daughter. In particular, the relationship between gifted females and their mothers emerges as an important factor. Reis found that gifted females whose mothers did not work outside the home struggled with the development of their own talents. The notion of becoming so different from their mothers caused tension and anxiety. Unfortunately, few notable role models for gifted females exist to ease their fears (Silverman, 1995).

Gifted girls may also struggle to achieve a balance between satisfying their intellectual needs and developing their social relationships. During adolescence, gifted girls shift from focusing on achievement needs to relationship needs. Kerr (1994) noted that, as a result of society's portrayal of the impossibility of balancing both successful careers and strong relationships, gifted adolescent females focus more on their relationships than they do on their achievement. Likewise, Silverman (1995) described the situation facing gifted adolescent girls as a "Sophie's Choice":

If she chooses to be true to herself, to honor her drive for achievement and self-actualization, she breaks some unspoken rule and faces disconnection, taunts, and rejection from both male and female peers. If she chooses to give up her dreams, to hold herself back, to redirect her energies into the feminine spheres—preoccupation with boys, clothes, appearance . . . she is accepted and rewarded for her efforts. (p. 146)

Silverman concluded that, since little immediate value can be seen in choosing achievement over social acceptance, gifted adolescent females need strong self-assurance to follow that path.

In addition to social relationships with peers, gifted women may also struggle to achieve a balance between their families' needs—their children, husband, and parents—and their own needs. Gilligan (1982) noted that women often make decisions and choices under an ethic of caring, which becomes problematic when it leads gifted females to sacrifice their own achievement goals and pursuits to meet others' needs, resulting in feelings of disappointment and regret (Callahan, Cunningham, & Plucker, 1994). When some gifted women reach middle age and the responsibility of caring for their children diminishes, they are able to find more time for creative productivity. However, as Reis (1999) indicated, some gifted middle-aged females are also finding themselves with the added responsibility of taking care of their aging parents, which may prevent them from finding time necessary for creative endeavors. Thus, throughout their lifetime, gifted females face a continual struggle between caring for and meeting the needs of family members and pursuing their own goals and aspirations.

Achievement and Underachievement Issues

While some gifted young women may place tremendous pressure on themselves to do it all and have it all, underachievement remains a prevalent problem facing many gifted females (Reis, 1999). For example, in her longitudinal study of high school valedictorians, Arnold (1993, 1994) reported that, of those continuing in science fields, only the women in the study stopped at the master's level or entered allied health fields such as nursing and physical therapy. On the other hand, the male valedictorians pursuing science went on to earn their medical or doctoral degrees in science fields.

Numerous explanations for the underachievement of gifted females have been offered. One explanation includes the pressure gifted females may feel to achieve in multiple domains. They may attempt to fulfill many different roles such as high-achieving student, star athlete, class officer, and participant in multiple extracurricular activities (Callahan et al., 1994). Gifted young women often want to have it all and do it all, yet this way of thinking is not free of consequences. Stress, burnout, and health problems are a few of the observed costs associated with the "superwoman" approach to life (Hollinger, 1991). Although gifted females frequently engage in multiple roles, they often are not taught how to manage and balance them (Callahan et al.).

One factor influencing underachievement in gifted females is a lack of future planning. Gifted females often excel in a number of areas, and this multipotentiality inhibits their ability to focus on a particular career path (Kerr, 1994). Research indicated that, when asked about their future plans, young men were likely to give specific career goals, whereas girls were not (Reis, Callahan, & Goldsmith, 1996). Further exacerbating the situation is evidence that significant adults in the lives of gifted females may not encourage them to think about long-term career goals (Callahan et al., 1994). Without adult role models encouraging and guiding them, gifted females may fail to gain direction and focus, thereby leaving their talents underdeveloped.

Underachievement in gifted young women may also be influenced by low self-efficacy and a lack of self-confidence. Noble (1989) reported that half of the women in her study cited self-doubt as the major reason for changing their career goals and the primary obstacle preventing them from developing their talents. This lack of confidence was also highlighted in a study of gifted adolescent females involved in the Westinghouse Talent Search. Subotnik (1988) noted that the young women involved in the science competition tended to credit their success to their efforts, rather than their intelligence and creativity. To stop the pattern of underachievement, gifted females must gain confidence in themselves and their abilities.

Resilience

In order to actualize their potential, gifted females need to develop psychological resilience to weather factors that threaten to stymie their achievement (Noble, 1996). Every female shares one obstacle to achievement in common: their cultivation by society into conventional gender-appropriate molds (Kline & Short, 1991). Other females, however, face additional adversities that may thwart their achievement, including poverty, racial discrimination, and dysfunctional families.

According to Noble (1996), gifted females need to develop resilience by adolescence so they can continue responding to their own goals, which may require resisting traditional notions of feminine "goodness" at a time when their relationships with others may discourage them from developing the characteristics of self-sufficiency and independence necessary for achievement. Gifted females must be prepared to face the potential ridicule, criticism, and isolation that may result from their decision to reject a traditional female lifestyle in pursuit of their own goals. Teenage girls who fail to form a shell of resilience against these negative forces often experience increased levels of self-doubt, depression, fear, and feelings of discouragement and hopelessness, all of which negatively impact the actualization of their abilities (Kline & Short, 1991).

Overcoming the effects of living in an impoverished environment plagued by poverty presents a major challenge to some gifted females. According to Seely (1993), intergenerational poverty results in lower parental expectations of children, lower educational levels of family members, and poorer general health, all of which can adversely affect the development of children's gifts and talents. Often, children reared in poverty are both perceived and treated as "losers," receiving the message that they are inadequate and deficient. As a result, they begin to experience feelings of helplessness, dependency, and inferiority (Evans, 1993). Developing resilience can help gifted females thwart these barriers to their achievement so they can actualize their potential.

Young women of color may also endure the effects of institutional racism that occurs when they are denied access to opportunities available to others that would allow them to fulfill their potential (Kuykendall, 1992). Institutional racism manifests in school systems when Black and Hispanic students are enrolled in less-rigorous educational programs. Such racism creates an atmosphere in which culturally diverse young women often feel they cannot succeed (Kuykendall, 1989). Due to their heightened sensitivities, gifted students in particular are at risk of experiencing pain as the result of discrimination (Evans, 1993). Gifted minority females may need help in developing the resilience needed to overcome social roadblocks (Diaz, 1998; Hébert & Reis, 1999).

Gifted young women faced with adversity need help understanding how to turn the effect of their hardships into fuel for achievement. Larson and Csikszentmihalyi (1997) emphasized the importance of adolescents facing adversity to reinterpret their conflicts into life lessons that enable them to reach a new understanding of self and overcome their hardships. Goertzel, Goertzel, and Goertzel (1978) found evidence of this in examining the childhoods of 400 eminent individuals. Eighty-five percent of these individuals came from seriously troubled home environments, which was similar to the findings of Ochse's (1990) research on highly creative adults. Noble (1996) acknowledged that the development of resilience is neither a simple nor effortless process, as it requires practice and persistence, the honing of psychological attitudes and skills, the development of inner resources, and the discovery and expression of one's abilities.

The literature has indicated that issues of gender-role expectations, relationship-oriented problems, achievement and underachievement, and the need for resilience are concerns for gifted females. Given that gifted young women face these issues, it becomes critical for educators and counselors to assist them in dealing with these challenges.

Guiding Gifted Females Through Bibliotherapy

Books have long been recognized as valuable, effective tools to help young people solve personal problems and develop skills necessary for success in life. Bibliotherapy is defined as the use of reading to produce affective change and promote personality growth and development (Frasier & McCannon, 1981; Halsted, 1994; Lenkowsky, 1987). Bibliotherapy happens when intelligent young women see something of themselves in a biography, identify with the person whose life story is being presented, reflect on that identification, and undergo some emotional growth as a result of that reading experience. Biographies of women of achievement may offer young gifted females opportunities to develop insight into the unique challenges they face.

To clarify the appropriate use of bibliotherapy with young women in school, a distinction needs to be made between *clinical bibliotherapy* and *developmental bibliotherapy*. Clinical bibliotherapy involves psychotherapeutic methods used by skilled and licensed practitioners with individuals experiencing serious emotional problems. Developmental bibliotherapy refers to helping students in their normal health and development and is the focus of this chapter. One of the advantages of this approach is that teachers can identify the concerns of young women in their classrooms and address the issues before they become problems, providing students with knowledge of what to expect and examples of how other gifted young women have dealt with the same concerns.

The use of biographies and guided reading has long been recognized as a viable option for helping gifted adolescents address their concerns. In the 1920s, Leta Hollingworth, the founder of the Speyer School for highly gifted children in New York City, infused biographical studies into the school's English curriculum. Hollingworth (1926) noted that her students requested biographies as part of their standard curriculum. They found that biographies were interesting and inspirational and showed them how to maintain high aspirations. As a strong proponent of biography, Hollingworth explained:

> For many reasons, the study of biography would seem to be especially appropriate in the education of gifted children. For adjustment to life as they are capable of living it, they need information as to how persons have found adjustment, as to how careers are made and are related serviceably to civilization, and to all the various kinds of intellectual work required by the world in their day. (pp. 319–320)

Forty years following Hollingworth's seminal work with gifted students, Hildreth (1966) wrote convincingly of the value of biography for gifted students:

> The reading of biography is an illuminating experience in which young people meet personalities they would like to emulate. In biography the young reader comes to identify [her]self with persons of intelligence and learning. Reading about noble deeds may not of itself produce noble character, but such reading is undoubtedly a source of inspiration. The ambitious young person who is fond of reading finds enchantment in the lives of people who overcame obstacles to achievement through dint of hard effort. (pp. 380–381)

Why is Bibliotherapy Appropriate for Gifted Young Women?

The struggles are difficult for all girls during adolescence, a time filled with many new stresses. When gifted girls arrive at adolescence, their experience may be different because of high levels of emotionality and sensitivity that often accompany high intelligence, exacerbating stressful experiences of daily living (Piechowski, 1997). Addressing the emotional needs of gifted teenage girls is critical (Buescher, 1985; Halsted, 1994), and using appropriate biographical materials may serve as a significant catalyst in helping them through their adolescent struggles. Several researchers have indicated that biographies can captivate gifted young women emotionally, and the bibliotherapy process using biographical materials is well supported (Flack, 1992, 1999; Kolloff, 1998; Piirto, 1992). Collections of materials for such an approach have also been highlighted by Kerr (1994) and Reis and Dobyns (1991), and biographical materials for gifted minority females have been highlighted by Ford and Harris (1999).

The research indicates that gifted students, particularly gifted girls, are often voracious readers, thus addressing affective concerns through guided reading appeals to their love of literature. The reading preferences of young women also suggest that biographies are a natural choice for them. Langerman (1990) noted in her research on the boys' and girls' reading preferences that young females tend to delve into more literature describing relationships. Since biographies are often filled with discussions of the important relationships in the lives of the central figures, the use of biography is aligned with the reading interests of gifted young women.

Guided reading of biographies is a counseling approach that is also consistent with the empathic qualities of gifted young women. Their need to vicariously experience the feelings of others is addressed through delving into biographies rich with descriptions of the challenges, frustrations, and joys of successful women.

Biographies may also provide gifted young women additional benefits. Through biographies, they will be exposed to role models that may be absent in their immediate lives (Silverman, 1993). In addition, biographies also expose gifted girls to new ways of thinking and looking at the world around them. Biographies allow them to gain exposure to a variety of philosophical views of life; various liberal and conservative worldviews; and a diversity of socioeconomic backgrounds, religions, and cultures. Another important consideration for using biographies is the realistic quality of this genre of literature. Biographies provide realistic portrayals of women's lives, leaving great impressions and eye-opening inspirational messages for gifted females. Finally, biographies may offer gifted young women whose lives are filled with adversity practical strategies for developing resilience.

Strategies for Using Biographies With Gifted Young Women

Biographies and autobiographies can be shared with gifted young women in a variety of ways; however, what remains important is that the teacher or counselor is prepared to listen closely to the emotional responses. Girls tend to be comfortable with self-disclosure in discussions that address emotional issues (Papini, Farmer, Clark, Micka, & Barnett, 1990). A female facilitator of a young women's bibliotherapy session should find it easy to have young women share their experiences with each other in a same-sex discussion group. With the female teacher or counselor as facilitator modeling appropriate self-disclosure, the younger participants in the discussion should feel comfortable opening up and providing emotional support for each other as they discuss the struggles of the gifted women featured in the biographies. In any discussion, whether one-on-one or in a group setting, the goal is for the young women to share their feelings and listen closely to both themselves and each other. In a group setting, it is important that the young women leave the session having reached an awareness that others have experienced the same feelings they are facing. A group discussion should bring about the universality of experience—a feeling that "we are in this together."

Counselors or teachers interested in conducting bibliotherapy sessions with gifted young women may want to consider facilitating brown bag luncheons or a "young women's reading group" during a school lunch period. Such an approach allows for same-sex discussions to occur comfortably, and the young women involved may generate other issues that are troubling them. Those who have been successful in leading bibliotherapy sessions with gifted young women may also want to create a biography discussion club and eventually allow the young women to select the biographies read by the group.

The following strategies are suggested as possibilities for designing effective bibliotherapy experiences for gifted young women.

- *Teachers and counselors may want to organize bibliotherapy sessions according to a focused theme or issue across multiple biographies.* For instance, having gifted girls examine gender-role expectations in the lives of a gifted female athlete, professional career woman, or author may help to enlighten how one issue may have impacted gifted women's lives differently. Another suggestion is to consider focusing strictly on the selected chapters describing the childhood and adolescent years of the woman featured in the biography. Other possibilities for a focus might be an examination of the chapter describing the career years of the featured individual or other portions of the biography that might be most meaningful to the group of young women participating in the bibliotherapy session.

- *Supplementing the written biography with an audio-visual component may serve to enrich the experience for the young women involved in the discussion.* Therefore, teachers conducting bibliotherapy sessions may also want to combine the biography with a vignette from an available biographical videotape. In addition, teachers may also want to consider combining the biography with a guest speaker. Many young women may find it difficult to identify with the biographies of women whom they perceive as "larger than life." For this reason, it may be helpful to invite as guest speakers younger successful women from backgrounds similar to the female featured in the biography who may be at earlier stages of their self-actualization. For example, if young women are reading about the life of Supreme Court Justice Sandra Day O'Connor, an appropriate guest speaker for that group of readers might be a local attorney who could share her experiences as a member of the community.

- *Critical to the success of any bibliotherapy session is the inclusion of activities following the group's discussion of the book.* The therapeutic effect of the biography depends on the group discussion facilitated by the teacher, who provides follow-up activities such as reflective writing, role-playing, creative problem solving, music and art activities, or self-selected options for students to pursue individually (Hébert, 1995; Hébert & Furner, 1997). When presented in this way, bibliotherapy can be enjoyable while providing a time for solid introspection. For example, following the reading of a biography featuring a gifted female athlete who struggled with gender-role expectations, the females involved in the session might enjoy designing stickers for their school lockers as daily reminders that young women can succeed in a variety of roles.

- *Also critical to the success of a bibliotherapy lesson is designing a menu of questions for discussion.* Teachers and counselors will want to have a generated list of prepared discussion questions to pursue with the group. Along with a menu of thoughtful questions designed to elucidate the feeling responses of the young women, bibliotherapy session leaders will want to have key quotes or selected passages from the biography as prompts ready for use in the discussion.

- *Secondary teachers in English departments might also consider offering an elective course in gender issues through literature.* The course could infuse instructional units in the curriculum, focusing on biographies of gifted women of achievement, as well as biographies of gifted males. Such a course would offer opportunities for both young women and men to develop a cross-gender understanding of the issues faced by teenagers.

- *Inviting a school counselor to serve as a cofacilitator in discussions about biographies is an effective way to address the social/emotional concerns of gifted young women.* This is particularly effective if a teacher is trying this strategy alone and feels somewhat uncomfortable handling discussions about emotionally laden topics.

Suggested Biographies and Autobiographies

The following biographies and autobiographies are recommended for counseling gifted young women regarding issues thematically reviewed in this article. The biographical materials are presented alphabetically, and the issues addressed in using the specific biographies are highlighted in Figure 5.1.

Madeleine Albright: A Twentieth Century Odyssey
(Michael Dobbs, 1999)

This inspirational biography provides the personal account of the life of an influential political and social figure in contemporary American society, the first female Secretary of State. The author portrays Madeleine Albright's complicated and challenging experiences growing up as the daughter of an American diplomat in a family immersed in political and international relations. Dobbs describes Albright's attempts to fulfill her parents' high expectations, her struggles with body image as a young woman, and her relentless drive to achieve. Young women who place tremendous pressure on themselves to achieve will identify with Albright's story. Teachers and counselors of adolescent females will find this work useful, in that the author highlights Albright's early school and family experiences.

Name	Gender Barriers	Relationship	Achieve- ment Issues	Resilience
Madeleine Albright			•	
Erma Bombeck		•		
Sandra Cisneros	•	•		•
Rhonda Cornum	•		•	•
Amelia Earhart		•		
Lorraine Hansberry		•	•	
Charlayne Hunter-Gault		•	•	•
Barbara Jordan	•	•	•	
Rebecca Lobo	•			
Wilma Mankiller		•		•
Gwendolyn Parker	•		•	
Esmeralda Santiago		•		
Beverly Sills				•
Maria Tallchief			•	
Heather Whitestone			•	•

Table 5.1. **Dominant Themes for the Women in the Selected Biographies**

Erma Bombeck: A Life in Humor (Susan Edward, 1997)

Erma Bombeck, a housewife, became a nationally syndicated humor columnist for more than 32 years. Through her column and bestselling books, Erma charmed her readership with her sassy irreverence for long-held American traditions, tempered by delightful good humor. Throughout her life and career, she was forever growing and learning, and she shared what she learned as wife and mother with millions of American women who learned and laughed along with her.

This biography is a celebration of a triumphant life sprinkled with the warm, wise, and potent wit that was uniquely Erma. Gifted young women will be able to reflect on many issues in her life that will enlighten their understanding of talent development in gifted females. Erma Bombeck's experiences with teachers who told her she had no talent as a writer and her eventual connection to a university English professor who recognized her abilities and provided her with encouragement and mentoring may have a profound effect on many intelligent young girls. Also important in this biography are the lessons young women may learn concerning the balancing of marriage, motherhood, and career.

She Went to War: The Rhonda Cornum Story (Rhonda Cornum and Peter Copeland, 1992)

This book offer gifted females a thrilling account of a remarkable female army physician. In the middle of a medical rescue mission during the Persian Gulf war, Cornum's helicopter was shot down. One of three survivors, she was immediately captured by Saddam Hussein's Republican Guard. What follows is a detailed account of Cornum's enduring spirit and resilience as she withstood harsh wartime imprisonment and badgering interrogations under the strain of severe, untreated injuries.

Mixed within the account of her wartime experiences is a depiction of Cornum's life history. Growing up a tomboy, Cornum faced criticism for her nontraditional interests when she decided to earn her doctoral degree in biochemistry. When she completed medical school and became a physician for the army, she found herself in the minority once again as one of few females to hold this position. As she dealt with pressure to prove her qualifications, she also focused on maintaining a balance between her career and family responsibilities. In reading Rhonda Cornum's life story, gifted young women will admire her unbreakable sprit, optimism, humor, and love of life.

East to the Dawn: The Life of Amelia Earhart (Susan Butler, 1997)

This biography of Amelia Earhart offers gifted females a realistic account of the struggles Amelia faced before achieving notoriety for her talent in aviation. Like many children, Amelia's family life was problematic, including an alcoholic father who squandered the family's money. A resilient woman, Amelia was able to thrive academically and socially despite these burdens. Gifted young women will easily identify with Amelia's difficulty in dealing with her multipotentiality. Unknown to many, Earhart did not always aspire to become a pilot. She donned many hats, including those of educator, social worker, lecturer, businesswoman, and feminist. Butler's biography provides gifted young women with a strong example of a multitalented woman with the courage and persistence to become a pioneer in a traditionally male-dominated field.

Sandra Cisneros: Latina Writer and Activist
(Caryn Mirriam-Goldberg, 1998)

This biography relates the story of Sandra Cisneros' struggle to find her identity and be understood by her peers. Growing up in a poor neighborhood in Chicago with prolonged visits to extended family in Mexico, Cisneros searched to find a balance between her Mexican and American heritages. The book also highlights the social difficulties Cisneros faced through adolescence and her perception of herself as an ugly duckling. Thinking she was completely unattractive to young men, she continued to have difficulty relating to her peers in college. While attending the University of Iowa's Writer's Workshop, she felt isolated because no other participants shared her experience of growing up in an impoverished environment.

Caryn Mirriam-Goldberg illustrates how Cisneros came to terms with her heritage by pursuing her talent as a writer. Cisneros, now an award-winning author, continues to publish poetry and serves as an activist encouraging other Latinas to reach their potential. Gifted females who can identify with Cisneros' feelings of isolation and identity confusion may feel encouraged by her ability to resolve these conflicts through the use of her talents.

Lorraine Hansberry (Anne Cheney, 1984)

This biography paints a vivid picture of the short, but interesting life of the renowned African American playwright who wrote *A Raisin in the Sun*. Cheney describes Lorraine Hansberry's childhood as one of isolation, feelings of awkwardness, and introspection. As early as kindergarten, this gifted female used her outsider status to listen carefully to and observe others, which benefited her years later as a writer. The Hansberry home was filled with discussions hosted by her activist father with famous, educated, and influential African Americans who helped to shape the playwright's thinking. Lorraine learned early that success was expected of her. While she strove to please her father, she marveled at her mother's beauty and never felt she could measure up to her perfection. Like many intelligent, sensitive, and lonely, young women, Lorraine found companionship in her books. The teenager who felt awkward and lonely dealt with those insecurities by writing stories and poetry. She experienced bigotry at the University of Wisconsin, but she continued to excel in her favorite areas of study, including literature, philosophy, and history.

Cheney's work highlights the childhood and adolescent experiences that challenged Hansberry early on and later influenced her success in life. What makes Hansberry's story remarkable is her compassion, modesty, and sensitivity to the needs of others. Revealing the insecurities, troubling peer issues, and family pressures faced by this gifted artist, Lorraine Hansberry's story offers gifted females excellent biographical material through which they may develop self-understanding.

In My Place (Charlayne Hunter-Gault, 1992)

In My Place is the autobiography of Charlayne Hunter-Gault, the first African American woman to break the barrier of segregation at The University of Georgia. It retraces Hunter-Gault's life story from her birth in the deep South to the historic role she played in the civil rights movement. Her story highlights the courage and strong convictions she maintained while facing the brutal realities of segregation.

Hunter-Gault describes her experiences growing up in a nurturing family that encouraged her academic achievement and shaped her aspirations to become a journalist. She was taught early in life that she was equally deserving of the best, which helped her to cope with the loneliness and ostracism she experienced as a college student. In her biography, she identifies strong teachers, good friends, and a dignified father as forces that shaped her.

As a gifted young woman, she excelled academically, exhibited leadership that was recognized within her community, and maintained successful relationships with her peers. As a gifted professional woman, she enjoyed an outstanding career as an international award-winning journalist. *In My Place* reminds readers how the strength of family support, belief in self, and persistence enables one to overcome adversity in life. This quality work emphasizes the significance of women developing a strong self-identity and resilience and offers significant implications for gifted young females who face seemingly insurmountable obstacles in the pursuit of their dreams.

Barbara Jordan: American Hero (Mary Beth Rogers, 1998)

This biography of Barbara Jordan provides gifted young women with an example of a resilient woman who overcame innumerable obstacles in her career as the first African American female senator in Texas, as well as the first Black woman elected to Congress from the South. Throughout her life, Jordan struggled in her relationship with her austere father, a Baptist minister with deep religious and moral standards to which he expected his daughter to adhere. While she enjoyed success and high achievement in high school and college, Jordan struggled academically when she attended Boston University Law School. Suddenly a small fish in a big pond, she discovered how her educational background had not adequately prepared her to compete in such an intense atmosphere.

With courage and strong dedication to her studies, Jordan was able to overcome the obstacles in her path, including the effects of racism and sexism. Rogers' biography follows Jordan through her political career as a senator and member of the United States Congress while she silently coped with multiple sclerosis and eventually leukemia. This biography will offer educators and counselors working with gifted young women excellent material for discussion that focuses on such important concerns as peer relations, parental expectations, body image issues, and gender-role expectations.

The Home Team: Of Mothers, Daughters and American Champions
(RuthAnn and Rebecca Lobo, 1996)

This autobiographical work, coauthored by a mother and daughter, is the story of one of our country's most prominent ambassadors for women's athletics. Now a player for the New York Liberty team, Rebecca Lobo is the most recognized and celebrated talent women's basketball has ever experienced. After leading the University of Connecticut's women's team to an undefeated season and the 1995 NCAA title, Rebecca went on to receive numerous prestigious athletic awards. RuthAnn Lobo is the woman who taught Rebecca that she could be a champion. The mother of three grown children, a guidance counselor, and educator, RuthAnn raised her daughter to envision new options for women without losing sight of her values.

Through alternating chapters in this mother-daughter autobiography, the Lobo women reflect on the joys and sufferings of growing up gifted and female. Rebecca shares her experiences growing up as a tomboy, heads taller than her schoolmates, playing basketball alone in her family driveway. Her mother recalls her own coming of age, reflecting on generational differences between her daughter's experiences and her own. Gender-role expectations are honestly discussed throughout the biography, and issues of femininity for female athletes are highlighted through insightful discussions by both authors. Rebecca describes her experiences with this issue, providing gifted females an important message in the following passage:

One thing I've never questioned is my femininity. No matter how my makeup and hair looked, I always felt very comfortable with myself, even in "boys' clothes". . . Whatever femininity is, it doesn't have anything to do with how much you weigh or how popular you are with boys. It would, of course, be best if we didn't have to confront such questions at all, if we could be as oblivious to them as the men's basketball team seems to be. I would tell my hypothetical little sister, If people on the outside question you, don't let it bother you. Just put their questions out of your head. Hopefully, people will start to realize that you can be an athlete and a woman. Women are out there proving that every day. (p. 78)

Along with such healthy discussion of gender-role expectations, another important theme in this biography is RuthAnn Lobo's successful battle to overcome cancer. Rebecca writes about her fear of losing her mother and about the enormous strength her mother's courage gave her. RuthAnn, in turn, shares her own fear of dying and her rediscovery and renewal of her religious faith. Sprinkled with a mother's wisdom and her gifted daughter's determination, *The Home Team* is an inspirational story about the power of two courageous women and their victories on and off the basketball court. By reading this biography, gifted females can learn the techniques of discipline and the joy of accomplishing at their highest potential.

Wilma Mankiller: A Chief and Her People (Wilma Mankiller, 1993)

Wilma Mankiller's autobiography is a story of resilience and strength. The first principle female chief of the Cherokee Nation of Oklahoma, Wilma Mankiller grew up in a large, poverty-stricken family. She describes the racism and ridicule she endured throughout her childhood following her family's move from the Indian reservation in Oklahoma to San Francisco, where she was mocked constantly by her peers for her last name and accent. Throughout adolescence, she continued to experience feelings of isolation and loneliness. As she grew older, she began to channel her energies into preserving the rights of the Cherokee Indians and was eventually nominated for Chief of the Cherokee nation. As she led her people both spiritually and politically, she continued to exemplify strength and resilience, overcoming profound hardships including a near-fatal car accident and kidney disease. The story of Wilma Mankiller offers gifted young women a powerful example of female leadership and a gifted woman's undying spirit.

Trespassing: My Sojourn in the Halls of Privilege (Gwendolyn M. Parker, 1997)

This is the autobiographical story of Gwendolyn Parker, a

successful African American woman and her journey through childhood, her experiences attending Ivy League educational institutions, and her fast-track career as a lawyer on Wall Street. Throughout her autobiography, Parker provides her readers with a vivid picture of her experiences growing up in Durham, North Carolina, in an educated, middle-class family that imposed a personal mandate on her to achieve excellence in life. Her family later moved to Mount Vernon, New York, where she learned through her difficult peer relations that the things that bound the Black community in Durham did not apply to her new home. Parker poignantly describes being shunned and called names such as "Miss Smartypants" by some of her Black peers as she gained success as a student.

Parker provides a close examination of her significant experiences breaking gender and racial barriers throughout her education, as well as in her career. As a teenager, she integrated the Kent School, a private boarding school in Connecticut, where she excelled academically, athletically, and in the school's theater. She went on to Radcliffe College and later New York University Law School. While completing her law degree, Parker was recruited by a conservative Wall Street law firm, where she became the only African American female member of the firm, an organization that rarely hired women. She described her difficulty making connections with others despite her attempts and the devastating lack of acceptance by her colleagues. She left the firm to work for American Express, where she served as director of a division for 8 years. In 1986, Parker resigned from her position, or, as she describes it, she "finally let go." Today, Parker does what she has always enjoyed doing: she writes novels. In bibliotherapy sessions with intelligent young women, teachers and counselors will find it easy to use Parker's powerful messages about coping with difficult peer relations, multipotentiality, gender barriers, and high parental expectations.

When I Was Puerto Rican (Esmeralda Santiago, 1993)

Gifted females will appreciate Esmeralda Santiago's coming-of-age autobiography. Santiago, a graduate of both the New York School of Performing Arts and Harvard University, endured many hardships as a young Puerto Rican girl. The eldest of seven children, she grew up in an impoverished environment trying to understand her parents' love/hate relationship and her father's infidelity. Santiago describes her frequent transitions to different neighborhoods and schools and finally her parents' separation and the family's move to New York. In the city, Esmeralda felt like an outsider in a foreign culture, and her inability to relate to her peers resulted in feelings of isolation and loneliness.

Santiago narrates the story in a simple style, relating the often heartbreaking events of her childhood gently and without judgment. Though it is one story of a strong individual, it provides insights into the formation of identity and talent development of culturally diverse females.

Beverly: An Autobiography
(Beverly Sills and Lawrence Linderman, 1987)

In this biography, readers learn how important it is to fall in love with an idea, the process by which creative women choose their life's work. Throughout Beverly Sills' life story, readers obtain an intimate view of the internationally renowned opera singer's passion for music and performing before audiences, which began when Beverly was a young girl singing on live radio broadcasts. An important theme in Sills' biography is the role of mentors who nurtured her gift and shaped her experiences as an opera singer. Her family relationships also strongly impacted her achievement as she internalized their beliefs and values regarding her ability to succeed. Gifted young women dealing with high parental expectations will appreciate the struggle between her mother's views and her father's views of their daughter's talent development and career. After being offered a national Broadway tour contract, Beverly's parents' expectations for her were severely at odds with each other. She described this struggle saying, "Mother and I were thrilled; Papa wasn't. Nice young women didn't go on the stage, they went to school, he said. If I went on the tour, I'd have to drop out of [school]. My mother stood up to him" (p. 30).

Sills also speaks to gifted young women who struggle with adversity. Beverly had two children, and shortly after the birth of her second child, she learned that her daughter was profoundly deaf and her son was severely retarded. When faced with personal difficulties, she worked harder, avoided self-pity, and maintained great emotional strength. As chairperson for the Mother's March on Birth Defects, she took her role seriously, celebrating it as one of her most rewarding challenges. In this biography, readers will appreciate Beverly Sills as a strong female who decided to live life to the fullest. Gifted young women will be inspired by the story of a talented and resilient female who balanced marriage, family, and a demanding career while coping with the adversities in her life.

Maria Tallchief: America's Prima Ballerina (Maria Tallchief, 1997)

The Native American ballerina Maria Tallchief shares in her autobiography exciting professional experiences as the prima ballerina in the New York City Ballet Company. In her work with George Balanchine, one of the greatest choreographers of all time, she created exhilarating roles requiring unlimited stamina and technical perfection. Though her life and career seemed glamorous, her honest discussion of her experiences offers gifted young women a realistic portrayal of the dedication and commitment necessary to cultivate talent. Maria poignantly describes how, at 17, she found herself thrust into the adult world of professional ballet, a world filled with rigorous training schedules and sacrifice and in which she managed to succeed in maintaining a balance among a demanding career, romantic relationships, and, eventually, motherhood.

Yes, You Can Heather!: The Story of Heather Whitestone, Miss America 1995 (Daphne Gray, with Gregg Lewis, 1995)

Listening With My Heart
(Heather Whitestone, with Angela Elwell Hunt, 1998)

For educators and counselors interested in leading guided reading discussions focused on issues of resilience in women's lives, two biographies on the life of Heather Whitestone may prove inspirational.

In *Yes, You Can Heather!: The Story of Heather Whitestone, Miss America 1995*, Heather's mother, Daphne Gray provides a heart-warming story of raising a profoundly deaf, gifted daughter. During the 1994 Miss America Pageant, Heather Whitestone challenged the limits of her deafness to capture both the pageant crown and America's heart.

Whitestone's dramatic story began 20 years earlier. At 18 months, Whitestone fell victim to a deadly illness that left her with a devastating hearing loss. During those dark days, her parents were faced with many difficult choices about their daughter's health, hearing, and education, choices that would dramatically affect their entire family's life. In this moving biography, Whitestone's mother recounts those extremely difficult choices. Refusing to leave her daughter in a silent world, she enrolled her in a ballet class. She researched the educational options for her daughter, making the controversial decision to emphasize speech, rather than sign language, and she never stopped believing that her daughter could strive in a hearing person's world. *Yes, You Can Heather!* is the inspiring story of Miss America 1995, but it is also the moving story of a mother who had to make agonizing choices and incredible sacrifices to enable her gifted, deaf daughter to achieve her dream.

In addition to Daphne Gray's biographical work, Heather Whitestone's autobiography *Listening With My Heart* is an important contribution to the literature available to gifted young women. Whitestone captivates her readers by telling her own story and the stories of others who have inspired her, proving that, with hard work and faith, young women can overcome adversity. This gifted, resilient young woman refused to listen to the voices of discouragement and instead followed the encouraging spirit of her family and the guidance of her heart. *Listening With My Heart* is filled with passages that will inspire gifted females and provide wonderful material for teachers and counselors to use in bibliotherapy discussions. One such passage highlights Heather's resilience during an experience in high school:

> Once, sitting in the classroom at Berry [High School] I remember being smitten with jealousy as I watched one of the popular girls laughing with her friends. At that moment, I would have given anything to have switched places with her, but I knew I couldn't. Even though I would have never wanted to give up my ballet, I always

wanted to be a homecoming queen or a cheerleader—
something that would have made me feel accepted by
everyone and maybe even admired. It was very difficult
for me to feel left out of the life everyone seemed to
share. One day I told myself, "I'll prove to them that
I'm something. I will find something better than popularity, more outstanding than cheerleading." (pp.
29–30)

Conclusion

During their journey into adulthood, gifted young women
frequently face important social and emotional issues that influence whether or not they achieve their full potential. This chapter
has explored issues of gender-role expectations, relationship-oriented problems, achievement and underachievement, and the
need for resilience that intelligent young women experience.
Teachers and counselors using biographies to counsel gifted middle and high school girls may find success addressing these concerns through bibliotherapy sessions. In the implementation of
such an approach to counseling, educators should consider that
addressing the important issues highlighted in this chapter may
empower gifted girls to seek their own unique educational pursuits, career aspirations, and life goals. It remains critical that educators support gifted young women in their exploration of their
goals and assist them in achieving their full potential.

Biographies and Autobiographies for Use With Gifted Girls

Butler, S. (1997). *East to the dawn: The life of Amelia Earhart*. Reading,
MA: Addison-Wesley.

Cheney, A. (1984). *Lorraine Hansberry*. Boston: Twayne.

Cornum, R., & Copeland, P. (1992). *She went to war: The Rhonda
Cornum story*. Novato, CA: Presidio.

Dobbs, M. (1999). *Madeleine Albright: A twentieth century odyssey*.
New York: Holt.

Edwards, S. (1997). *Erma Bombeck: A life in humor*. New York: Avon.

Gray, D., & Lewis, G. (1995). *Yes, you can Heather!: The story of Heather
Whitestone, Miss America 1995*. Grand Rapids, MI: Zondervan.

Hunter-Gault, C. (1992). *In my place.* New York: Farrar Strauss Giroux.

Lobo, R. A., & Lobo, R. (1996). *The home team: Of mothers, daughters, and American champions.* New York: Kodansha International.

Mankiller, W. (1993). *Wilma Mankiller: A chief for her people.* New York: St. Martin's Press.

Mirriam-Goldberg, C. (1998). *Sandra Cisneros: Latina writer and activist.* Springfield, NJ: Enslow.

Parker, G. (1997). *Trespassing: My sojourn in the halls of privilege.* Boston: Houghton Mifflin.

Rogers, M. B. (1998). *Barbara Jordan: American hero.* New York: Bantam.

Santiago, E. (1993). *When I was Puerto Rican.* New York: Random House.

Sills, B., & Linderman, L. (1987). *Beverly: An autobiography.* New York: Bantam.

Tallchief, M. (1997). *Maria Tallchief: America's prima ballerina.* New York: Holt.

Whitestone, H., & Hunt, A. E. (1998). *Listening with my heart.* New York: Doubleday.

References

Arnold, K. D. (1993). The lives of female high school valedictorians in the 1980s. In K. D. Hurlbert & D. T. Schuster (Eds.), *Women's lives through time: Educated American women of the twentieth century* (pp. 393–414). San Francisco: Jossey Bass.

Arnold, K. D. (1994). The Illinois Valedictorian Project: Early adult careers of academically talented male high school students. In R. F. Subotnik & K. D. Arnold (Eds.), *Beyond Terman: Contemporary longitudinal studies of giftedness and talent* (pp. 24–51). Norwood, NJ: Ablex.

Bakken, L., Hershey, M., & Miller, P. (1990). Gifted adolescent females' attitudes toward gender equality in educational and intergender relationships. *Roeper Review, 12,* 261–264.

Buescher, T. (1985). A framework for understanding the social and emotional development of gifted and talented adolescents. *Roeper Review, 8,* 10–15.

Callahan, C. M. (1979). The gifted and talented woman. In A. H. Passow (Ed.), *The gifted and talented* (pp. 401–423). Chicago: National Society for the Study of Education.

Callahan, C. M., Cunningham, C. M., & Plucker, J. A. (1994). Foundations for the future: The socio-emotional development of gifted, adolescent women. *Roeper Review, 17,* 99–105.

Callahan, C. M., & Reis, S. M. (1996). Gifted girls, remarkable women. In K. D. Arnold, K. D. Noble, & R. F. Subotnik (Eds.), *Remarkable women: Perspectives on female talent development* (pp. 171–192). Cresskill, NJ: Hampton Press.

Diaz, E. I. (1998). Perceived factors influencing the academic underachievement of talented students of Puerto Rican descent. *Gifted Child Quarterly, 42,* 105–122.

Evans, K. (1993). Multicultural counseling. In L. K. Silverman (Ed.), *Counseling the gifted and talented* (pp. 277–290). Denver: Love.

Flack, J. D. (1992). *Lives of promise: Studies in biography and family history.* Englewood, CO: Teacher Idea Press.

Flack, J. D. (1999). *Autobiography and gifted students: Hows and whys.* Storrs: Confratute: Summer Institute on Enrichment Learning and Teaching, University of Connecticut.

Ford, D. Y. (1995). Underachievement among gifted and non-gifted Black females: A study of perceptions. *Journal of Secondary Gifted Education, 6,* 165–175.

Ford, D. Y., & Harris, J. J. III. (1999). *Multicultural gifted education.* New York: Teachers College Press.

Frasier, M. M., & McCannon, C. (1981). Using bibliotherapy with gifted children. *Gifted Child Quarterly, 25,* 81–84.

Gilligan, C. (1982). In a different voice: Psychological theory and women's development. Cambridge, MA: Harvard University Press.

Goertzel, M. G., Goertzel, V., & Goertzel, T. G. (1978). *Three hundred eminent personalities.* San Francisco: Jossey-Bass.

Halsted, J. W. (1994). *Some of my best friends are books: Guiding gifted readers from pre-school to high school.* Dayton: Ohio Psychology Press.

Hébert, T. P. (1995). Using biography to counsel gifted young men. *Journal of Secondary Gifted Education, 6,* 208–219.

Hébert, T. P., & Furner, J. M. (1997). Helping high-ability students overcome math anxiety through bibliotherapy. *Journal of Secondary Gifted Education, 8,* 164–178.

Hébert, T. P., & Reis, S. M. (1999). Culturally diverse high-achieving students in an urban high school. *Urban Education, 34,* 428–457.

Hildreth, G. H. (1966). *Introduction to the gifted.* New York: McGraw-Hill.

Hollinger, C. (1991). Career choices for gifted adolescents: Overcoming stereotypes. In M. Bireley & J. Genshaft (Eds.), *Understanding the gifted adolescent: Educational development and multicultural issues* (pp. 201–214). New York: Teachers College Press.

Hollingworth, L. S. (1926). *Gifted children: Their nature and nurture.* New York: Macmillan.

Johnson, M. (1997, September). Oprah Winfrey: A life in books. *Life*, 44–60.

Kerr, B. (1994). *Smart girls: A new psychology of girls, women and gift-edness*. Scottsdale, AZ: Gifted Psychology Press.

Kitano, M. K. (1995). Lessons from gifted women of color. *Journal of Secondary Gifted Education, 6,* 176–187.

Kline, B. E., & Short, E. B. (1991). Changes in emotional resilience: Gifted adolescent females. *Roeper Review, 13,* 118–121.

Kolloff, P. B. (1998, November). *Lessons from gifted lives.* Paper presented at the annual meeting of the National Association for Gifted Children, Louisville, KY.

Kuykendall, C. (1989). *Improving Black student achievement by enhancing student self-image.* Washington, DC: American University, Mid-Atlantic Equity Center.

Kuykendall, C. (1992). *From rage to hope: Strategies for reclaiming Black and Hispanic students.* Bloomington, IN: National Education Service.

Langerman, D. (1990, March). Books and boys: Gender preferences and book selection. *School Library Journal,* 132–136.

Larson, R., & Csikszentmihalyi, M. (1997). The growth of complexity: Shaping meaningful lives. *NAMTA Journal, 22,* 176–195.

Lenkowsky, R. S. (1987). Bibliotherapy: A review and analysis of the literature. *Journal of Special Education, 21,* 123–132.

Mann, J. (1994). *The difference: Growing up female in America.* New York: Warner.

Noble, K. D. (1987). The dilemma of the gifted woman. *Psychology of Women Quarterly, 11,* 367–378.

Noble, K. D. (1989). Counseling gifted women: Becoming the heroes of our own stories. *Journal for the Education of the Gifted, 12,* 131–141.

Noble, K. D. (1996). Resilience, resistance, and responsibility: Resolving the dilemma of the gifted woman. In K. D. Arnold, K. D. Noble, & R. F. Subotnik (Eds.), *Remarkable women: Perspectives on female talent development* (pp. 413–423). Cresskill, NJ: Hampton.

Ochse, R. (1990). *Before the gates of excellence: The determinants of creative genius.* Cambridge, United Kingdom: Cambridge University Press.

Papini, D. R., Farmer, F. F., Clark, S. M., Micka, J. C., & Barnett, J. K. (1990). Early adolescent age and gender differences in patterns of emotional self-disclosure to parents and friends. *Adolescence, 25,* 959–976.

Piechowski, M. M. (1997). Emotional giftedness: The measure of intrapersonal intelligence. In N. Colangelo & G. A. Davis (Eds.),

Handbook of gifted education (2nd ed., pp. 366–381). Needham Heights, MA: Allyn and Bacon.

Piirto, J. (1991). Why are there so few? (Creative women: visual artists, mathematicians, musicians). *Roeper Review, 13,* 142–147.

Piirto, J. (1992). *Understanding those who create.* Dayton: Ohio Psychology Press.

Reis, S. M. (1999). *Work left undone: Choices and compromises of talented women.* Mansfield Center, CT: Creative Learning Press.

Reis, S. M., & Callahan, C. M. (1989). Gifted females. They've come a long way—or have they? *Journal for the Education of the Gifted 12,* 99–117.

Reis, S. M., Callahan, C. M., & Goldsmith, D. (1996). Attitudes of adolescent gifted girls and boys toward education, achievement, and the future. In K. D. Arnold, K. D. Noble, & R. F. Subotnik (Eds.), *Remarkable women: Perspectives on female talent development* (pp. 209–224). Cresskill, NJ: Hampton Press.

Reis, S. M., & Dobyns, S. M. (1991). An annotated bibliography of non-fictional books and curricular materials to encourage gifted females. *Roeper Review, 13,* 129–134.

Rimm, S. B., Rimm-Kaufman, S., & Rimm, I. (1999). *See Jane win: The Rimm report on how 1,000 girls became successful women.* New York: Crown.

Sadker, M., & Sadker, D. (1994). *Failing at fairness: How America's schools cheat girls.* New York: Charles Scribner's Sons.

Seeley, K. (1993). Gifted students at risk. In L. K. Silverman (Ed.), *Counseling the gifted and talented* (pp. 263–275). Denver: Love.

Silverman, L. K. (1993). Social development, leadership, and gender issues. In L. K. Silverman (Ed.), *Counseling the gifted and talented* (pp. 291–327). Denver: Love.

Silverman, L. K. (1995). To be gifted or feminine: The forced choice of adolescence. *Journal of Secondary Gifted Education, 6,* 141–156.

Subotnik, R. F. (1988). The motivation to experiment: A study of gifted adolescents' attitudes toward scientific research. *Journal for the Education of the Gifted, 11*(3), 19–35.

Subotnik, R. F., & Arnold, K. D. (1996). Success and sacrifice: The cost of talent fulfillment for women in science. In K. D. Arnold, K. D. Noble, & R. F. Subotnik (Eds.), *Remarkable women: Perspectives on female talent development* (pp. 263–280). Cresskill, NJ: Hampton Press.

chapter 7

Life Strategies of Five Wives, Mommies, and Scientists

by **Juanita Jo Matkins** *and* **Rhea Miles**

hatever the definition used for giftedness, there should be no question about the gifts of women who achieve the highest levels of success in areas of science. Renzulli (1978) argued that there were three important aspects of giftedness: creativity, task commitment, and a high level of intelligence. The women discussed in this chapter were all Ph.D. recipients in an area of science, and they were each remarkable in their particular field. The execution of many of the routine tasks in each science discipline employed the very qualities of giftedness cited by Renzulli, and the achievements of these five women showed that they brought energy, insight, and fresh approaches to their science disciplines. In finding ways to incorporate the roles of wife and mother into their careers, these women exposed another possible facet to the dimensions of giftedness through the strategies they pioneered.

These five women represent a variety of science disciplines: meteorology, forensic pathology, physics, and astronomy (see Table 7.1).[1] The meteorologist, Libby, was the first female senior scientist at a major national atmospheric research facility. The forensic pathologist, Sophy, was chief medical examiner for her state. Carol, the astronaut/physicist, flew on several Space Shuttle missions, experienced several spacewalks, and served as mission commander. One of the astronomers, Florence, was a recipient of the Presidential Medal of Freedom and a member of the National Academy of Science. The other astronomer, Maria, was the first female to be awarded a tenured position in her university's astronomy department.

In addition to being a scientist, each of these remarkable women was also a wife and a mother, and this array of roles presented challenges for them. The strategies they used for meeting their challenges can be helpful to gifted individuals, parents, teachers, and others who have an impact on gifted girls.

A Few Glimpses

I sat in Sophy's office and asked her why she went back to work so soon after the birth of her two children. Her reply revealed the passion she felt for her profession and the hardheaded practicality she wielded when questioning gender stereotypes:

I had to go back to work. I wanted to go back to work. I knew I would be a much happier mother if I went back to work. And, when you're in a profession that is constantly changing, from day to day, you can't quit. You'd have to practically retrain.

On another day, I interviewed Florence, and she described a scene about a year after the birth of her first child. Her husband discovered her sitting alone in their living room, crying, and holding a magazine in her lap. As she described it:

I wept every time *The Astrophysical Journal* came into the house. I couldn't say those words until 5 years ago without weeping. I was so miserable knowing that other people were doing astronomy, and I was not. My husband understood this. We talked about it, and he said I should go back to school.

Table 7.1
Characteristics of Five Women Scientists

Woman Scientist	Career	Marital Status	Age	No. of Children	Exceptional Accomplishments
Libby	Meteorologist	Married	50	2	First female senior scientist at her institution
Sophy	Forensic Scientist	Married	54	2	Chief medical examiner
Carol	Astronaut/ Physicist	Married	44	2	Four Shuttle flights, Hubble Space Telescope repair
Florence	Astronomer	Married	68	4	National Medal of Science
Florence	Astronomer	Married	41	2	First tenured woman in her department

Libby was absent from work for weeks at a time and worked part-time for long stretches as she endured heart disease, gave birth to two children, and tended her mother until the inevitable end of terminal cancer. When asked to think about pivotal events in her life, Libby observed that the breaks in her work routine had actually enhanced her insight into her work. During the time she took off, she read Laura Ingalls Wilder's books and did jigsaw puzzles. And, upon her return to research, she developed a new approach to understanding an important aspect of the physics of storms: the transport of momentum in squall lines. She suspected that this "going away" from the work was probably an advantage for women because she had been able to see fresh approaches to her work after being away from it.

Young women who are interested in a science career face societal, cultural, and academic factors that often disable their ability to persevere and achieve in the sciences. In *Educated in Romance*, Holland and Eisenhart (1990) found that most young college women assumed they would have to give up career aspirations in order to have a family. The pressures of the "sexual auction block" were sufficient to divert women during their college years into less-demanding academic regimens and accepting an arrangement where they "fit into" less-prestigious jobs than their husbands. Arnold (1993), in a longitudinal study of high school valedictorians and salutatorians, found that gifted women expected to have to marginalize themselves in exchange for having a family.

The idea that one must be successful by the age of 30, assumed in the sciences, complicates the life goals of many women who are talented in science. In a study of 11 women scientists, Subotnik and Arnold (1996) concluded that this sequence conflicts with the normative time frame of establishing families and developing family relationships. Thus, young women interested in science careers risk giving up what many consider to be the essential feminine roles of being a wife and a mother. Women who intend to have a family feel their biological clocks ticking, and science is an area where the ticking is very loud.

The five women scientists in this study were academically gifted and achieved recognition in their chosen fields (see Table 7.1). Accomplishments ranged from receiving the Presidential Medal of Freedom, to the repair of the Hubble Space Telescope. Aside from their professional accomplishments, it is of great significance that these five women were all married and had children; all found ways to reconcile the demands of home and career.

Seven Strategies for Successfully Balancing Career and Family

These women exhibited seven major strategies for dealing with the dilemmas presented by the multiple roles of wife, mother, and scientist. What follows are the strategies and some vignettes from their lives that can be used when talking with gifted girls about the difficulties and triumphs of juggling these different aspects of life.

1. Concentration in a subject because of its appeal to the individual.

Mysteries and problems, delving into the unknown, and the challenge of their studies were common denominators to explain the passion these women had for their science. Florence's research into the nature of dark matter originally generated disdain among the astronomical community, and her first papers were turned down by two leading journals in the field. She was convinced that there was a way to understand how the universe worked. Florence asked, "How could you be here and not attempt to understand these things? I just had some kind of a confidence that, if you worked hard enough, you could understand these things."

Carol liked the work she did in physics because it was hard.

> Physics seemed to be more of a puzzle. More of a challenge. If I had a German translation to do for homework, I knew about how long it would take. If I had physics problems, it would take 5 minutes or 5 hours. You never really knew which. It just depended upon how long it took for the concept to click in your brain. I've always liked problems, and it was just a big puzzle.

2. Acceptance of the need to work hard to master the subject and balance multiple roles.

Though these women were intensely absorbed with their studies, life had a way of intruding. Tragedy struck during Maria's first semester of college when her only sister died. She struggled with the intense yearlong courses in mathematics and physics required in the program and found the additional stress of her sister's death almost too much to cope with. Her final exam scores were not satisfactory, and she had to retake the exams after a summer devoted to intense study—a summer Maria recalled as one of the worst of her life. Her second tries were successful, and she was able to continue on the path she had charted for herself that led to being an astronomer.

When Sophy took organic chemistry the first time, she got a D in the first semester and a C the second semester, grades that would not get her into medical school. So, she took the two semesters of organic chemistry again over the next summer and got A's both sessions. "I had to have organic to get into medical school, and there wasn't any question that I had to take it over again. I had to master it." Once Sophy began practicing forensic pathology, she showed similar single-mindedness in balancing the roles of wife and mother with career.

For a lot of years, I only had two missions in life. One was to keep the house going and the other was to keep the office going. And that was it. I didn't belong to any social clubs or anything like that. I did my work, and, if I wasn't at work, I was at home.

3. Development of a strong sense of self.

The childhood stories of these five women foreshadow the self-confidence and goal-directed behavior that led to their later success and strong sense of their own worth and abilities.

Libby knew she wanted to be a meteorologist from the time she was in second grade and lightning struck her chimney, sending pieces of brick flying across the living room. She began keeping meticulous daily records of the weather in seventh grade. In the ninth grade, her teacher told her she should forget about meteorology and be a nurse like her mother, but Libby was not deterred. When she turned 16, her mother attempted to divert Libby from her ambitions by sending her to a Midwestern girls' school for a year to learn to be a "lady." It was there that Libby learned that the word *bookish*, applied to herself, wasn't intended to be complimentary. Libby was very unhappy, and upon her return and with the support of her mother, she skipped her senior year of high school and went straight into a meteorology program at a nearby college. Her finishing school experience had taught Libby to be an even stronger advocate for herself.

Sophy always knew she wanted to be some sort of scientist, and she read all the science books in her elementary school's library.

In many ways, it was easy for me. Once it became clear to me that my interest in science would be translated into medicine, life was a breeze. You always knew where you were going. I was lucky that I found medicine early on. I would've been a societal misfit. I also knew I was probably not going to sit home and have eight kids. I really didn't care that much for housework.

Sophy's assessment of her potential to become a societal misfit had she not found medicine as her goal is perhaps descriptive of the terrible situation endured by gifted women in previous generations. They lived with the stresses of the cultural demands for women to be docile, contrasted in painful ways with their own need for challenge.

4. Flexibility in timeframes for work and family.

Variations in traditional timeframes were commonplace for these women. Five years after her marriage, Carol moved to Houston, Texas, with her daughter, where she began training as an astronaut. Her husband remained in residence in the university town that was his home. For 12 years, Carol and her husband maintained a long-distance relationship, during which Carol flew four Space Shuttle missions and bore two more daughters. Even during Sophy's husband's stint in the Army during the Vietnam era, she lived on base with the children and worked part-time while he fulfilled his obligation to the U.S. armed forces.

Libby worked half-time when the children were little, going home for lunch to nurse each one. After heart surgery, she took an extended medical leave and returned to her research with fresh insights.

5. Choice of a husband with similar interests.

Libby and her husband met and became good friends while working together on a committee for their professional science organization. Carol married her major advisor a few weeks after graduating with a Ph.D. in physics. Maria met her husband during their studies together in the West Indies university near her home. They were married at the end of her first year of Ph.D. work in astronomy at a Canadian university. By the time she completed her studies, he was a tenured faculty member in mathematics at a university. Florence was introduced to her husband, a physics major, by her parents; they married when she completed her undergraduate degree. She completed her master's studies while he completed his Ph.D. at the same university. Sophy and her husband met as undergraduates and then went to medical school, but at universities in two different countries. Despite their long-distance romance, their commitment to each other continued, and they were married the day after Sophy graduated from medical school. Sophy did her internship while her husband finished medical school at the same teaching hospital.

6. Planning of pregnancy and childbirth around career needs.

A common characteristic of these five women was the forethought shown when they decided to take on the responsibility of motherhood. The availability of birth control, specifically the pill, was a crucial factor in Sophy's ability to maintain a balance between career and motherhood. She characterized a lack of birth control as "fertility roulette. Son of a gun, I might be pregnant." It could be catastrophic to both partners and a disservice to the child and the family. Recognizing this as one of the natural conflicts in living, Sophy felt little compunction in making the choice for herself, rather than leaving her motherhood to chance.

Two of Carol's three daughters were born while she was a NASA astronaut, and, because NASA astronauts cannot fly while pregnant, the pregnancies were carefully planned around training and missions. Libby and her husband wanted to have two children and to have those children within 5 years of being married. Both were well established in their careers, and they wanted to have a family, yet control the number and arrival of their children. They celebrated their fifth anniversary and the birth of their second child, which was followed by a tubal ligation.

Though Maria was entitled to a year's leave when her second child was born, she chose to return to work after 6 weeks. She had already taken an extended pregnancy-related leave and felt she needed to get back into the office.

Florence planned her four pregnancies, and she declared firmly that none of her children were accidents.

All five of these women made a conscious choice to have children, and each exhibited various strategies to time pregnancy and childbirth so that the impact on their work would be minimized. Their method for reconciling the roles of mother, wife, and scientist was to anticipate the consequences of motherhood and take advantage of opportunities to adapt their biological timeline to their career. Despite medical advances such as the birth control pill and tubal ligation, there remained professional pressures such as those felt by Maria and Sophy, who returned to work not only for personal satisfaction, but also to maintain their standing as serious scientists.

7. Anticipation of childcare needs and strategies to meet those needs.

Once parenthood was an actuality, the practicalities of childcare arrangements became a necessary part of the daily routine.

Carol's husband flew 1,500 miles to Houston as often as his schedule would permit. When her training and Shuttle missions necessitated long absences, he was in charge of the children. Her work as an astronaut "wouldn't have been possible if he wasn't as supportive as he is." During the years in Houston, Carol employed a full-time housekeeper/nanny who cared for the children and did housework when Carol could not be around. When the middle daughter suffered a severely broken leg while on a family ski trip, Carol took full responsibility for nursing her back to health. This meant evening and morning nursing, as well as leaving the Johnson Space Center during the day and driving several miles home to feed, turn, provide the bedpan, and otherwise minister to the needs of a reluctant and restless invalid.

Sophy employed various strategies in anticipation of needing childcare, including paying two other young mothers on the Army base to be on-call for childcare for her children. She reasoned, "If you're going to be a mother, the one thing you have to nail down is your childcare, or else you will go crazy. . . . Otherwise, you have crises, preventable crises." When discussing the expense of paying for childcare, Sophy rejoined,

> I always paid more than everyone else paid because you have to keep these people. Good childcare doesn't come cheap. The idea of paying an entry-level salary to an employee taking care of your child is nuts. Think about it. What are you paying for? You are paying for your surrogate. That's an investment. I never begrudged the money I paid for childcare.

Maria remembered feeling uncomfortable at having to leave departmental gatherings in order to get to the babysitter on time. She enjoyed being with her children, yet when she was with them, she felt guilty that she wasn't working on her research and her writing. When she was at work, she felt guilty she wasn't at home with the children. She went on to describe how she sometimes carried the stresses of the office home with her and yelled at her kids. Yet, she looked forward to going home and seeing them because it somewhat relieved the stresses of the day.

Libby had four children, two with her husband and two from her husband's first marriage. During the time she was nursing the two younger children, she attended professional meetings accompanied by her husband and her children. Her husband tended the children while she was in a session. Libby was on call during hurricane season since her research involved analysis of the genesis and structure of hurricanes. Her husband took all parenting responsibilities when she was in the field. She remembered getting calls that conditions were right and the airplane was being readied to fly into the hurricane, and her husband would say, "Okay, I'll take care of the kids. Bye!"

During the time Florence was developing the scholarship that led to her receiving the National Medal of Science for her work on the question of dark matter, she was also giving birth to and raising four children. She recalled times when she would be engrossed in working on calculations for her dissertation research; she would put the children to bed at 7:00 p.m., work until 2:00 a.m., go to sleep exhausted, and get up at 7:00 a.m. with the children.

> You have to have a life. I think maybe women are doing themselves a disservice. We all work, whether we're doing something ennobling or something horrible. You either have to scrub the floor or go to the telescope, and I'd much rather go to the telescope than scrub the floor.

Implications and Recommendations

There are common strategies and situations that allowed these women to resolve the conflicts of wife, mother, and scientist that should be shared with gifted girls interested in pursuing high-demand careers and having families at the same time.

- Each of the five women was married, and their husbands had professional interests that were similar to their wives'. The women described their husbands as their friends. Crucially, all the husbands actively participated in childcare. These women knew that it was hard to become and be a scientist and that it was exponentially harder to maintain a marriage, a family, and a career. They all coped successfully with tending infants, juggling graduate studies, doing part-time work, or starting a new job, and their husbands were essential to this success. There was no difference in the characteristics of the older women's husbands compared to the younger women's, leading to the conclusion that this was a factor across a range of women scientists and not just a phenomenon of a cultural change in acceptable behaviors in husbands and fathers.

- These five women employed effective birth control. The need for childcare was anticipated, and good childcare was valued and rewarded. Most of the women altered in some way the time they put into their profession during their child-rearing years. All considered their children to be part of their contribution; they agreed that the children mattered.

- These women reported that their professional work was satisfying. Several admitted that they were glad to return to work after the birth of their children. They needed to keep in contact with their work to stay current with developments in their field, and they needed to work in order to be sane.

- The rejection of cultural norms was common among these women. They were not amenable to conforming to external expectations; their personal goals were more important. There were hard choices to be made when societal, cultural, and professional expectations were opposed to their own preferences. Despite the perception that having children could put her chances of a secure faculty position at risk, Maria chose to become a mother. In order to be an astronaut, Carol chose to have three children and live more than

1,000 miles from her husband. Florence chose a lower paying job in order to do the research she wanted to do. Libby, Florence, and Carol chose work that kept them away from their families for extended periods. Sophy endured the criticism of others in medical school who said she should drop out and let a deserving male take her place.

- The ability of these women to be wives and mothers in their professions is inextricably entwined with their sense of themselves as scientists. These women chose their professions based upon their own preferences, often contradicting the advice of parents and well-meaning advisors. Florence was told there would be no jobs for astronomers during her studies in the pre-Sputnik years. Libby's mother wanted a nice daughter, not a tomboy with a passion for meteorology. Carol, Maria, and Sophy also exhibited their own focused intention.

Using the Stories to Work With Gifted Girls

Self-actualization as a woman scientist—the sense of possible-self-as-woman-scientist—can be achieved, and this must be shared with young gifted girls. The cases of the five women in this study show that there are certain strategies that were effective in becoming a woman scientist and in balancing professional obligations with those of being a wife and a mother.

The assumption that a woman cannot become a successful scientist while being a wife and mother implies the presumption that this combination will diminish one of the roles and that the predictable and conventional paths of the past are the only acceptable ones. The stories of these five women undermine that assumption: These are extremely successful women who experienced no diminishing of stature because of their multiple roles. Women who want to be scientists do not have to choose marriage and motherhood to be successful, but women should have the choice. The women detailed here made that choice—they embraced the difficulties inherent in all ambition, especially for those who are forging new cultural norms.

The strategies employed by these women are applicable to young women who are interested in pursuing a science career while having the option of also becoming wives and mothers. If there is a formula for success in science while pursuing a future as a wife and mother, it is this: Find what you're interested in, believe in yourself, work hard to learn your subject and, later, work hard in your research. Look for a lifemate with similar interests, who thinks you should pursue your career, and who will help you raise your children. Make your own life path and don't let societal norms dictate your choices. Set timelines that work for you. Plan ahead. Don't get pregnant until you're ready to have a baby. Anticipate childcare needs and put energy and resources into acquiring good childcare.

Parents and teachers of gifted girls and counselors who work with them can use the stories of these women as evidence that it is not necessary to deny traditional feminine roles if the career goal is to become a scientist. Girls with a sense of possible-self-as-a-scientist should be counseled by both teachers, parents, and counselors to challenge themselves academically in all subject areas, but particularly in mathematics and science. The transition from the self-image of a sense of possible-self-as-a-scientist to sense of possible-self-as-a-woman-scientist can be fostered and nurtured through exposure to role models such as the women detailed in this chapter. Teachers can point out the lack of lockstep maturational timelines in their stories: They married, had babies, did research, had health problems, nurtured others, and got on with their lives on schedules dictated by their own goals, not as a result of externally proposed milestones.

Their parents were especially important to these five gifted women. Parents should consider the deeper implications of the Sophy's words describing how she overcame all the obstacles: "Nobody told me I couldn't." This wasn't true. In Sophy's story, there were many people who told her she couldn't—nurses, professors, and members of the community. However, Sophy's mother never told her she couldn't, and that's what made the difference for her. Libby's mother tried to shape Libby into a debutante, but wisely recognized her mistake and became a staunch supporter of Libby's early transition from high school to college. There is much in gifted literature about the importance of role models external to the family. But, in the stories of these five women, parents were the strongest role models. Teachers working with gifted young women do well when they develop cooperative relationships with the parents of their students.

Together, teachers and parents can form a safety net for young women embracing the challenging world of science while working through the vicissitudes of emergent adulthood.

The stories of these women also point to strategies for research institutions, if these institutions are serious about increasing the number of woman scientists in their ranks. Flexibility in timelines for tenure and energetic recruiting of a cohort of women in a research area have the potential to give young women confidence that they can succeed in an institution's system. Conversely, departments and schools where childcare needs and pregnancy demands are treated with low regard may find themselves lacking female role models with which to recruit more women.

References

Arnold, K. D. (1993). Undergraduate aspiration and career outcomes of academically talented women: A discriminant analysis. *Roeper Review, 15,* 169–175.

Holland, D. C., & Eisenhart, M. A. (1990). *Educated in romance: Women, achievement and college culture.* Chicago: University of Chicago Press.

Renzulli, J. (1978). What makes giftedness?: Reexamining a definition. *Phi Delta Kappan, 60,* 180–184, 260.

Subotnik, R. F., & Arnold, K. D. (1996). Success and sacrifice: The costs of talent fulfillment for women in science. In K. Arnold, K. D. Noble, & R. F. Subotnik (Eds.), *Remarkable women; Perspectives on female talent development* (pp. 262–280). Cresskill, NJ: Hampton Press.

End Notes

1.   Participants granted permission for use of their information in the study, with the agreement that specific identities would be confidential and pseudonyms would be used. They were chosen through a process of purposeful sampling for science areas where women were still relatively rare: physics, the Earth sciences, and forensic medicine. Interviews were conducted over a 2-year period.

chapter 8

Actualized Women
*using the accomplishments
of highly able women to inspire gifted girls*

by **Jan B. Hansen** *and* **Eleanor G. Hall**

eneral consensus from gender equity research is that gifted girls are underrepresented in the vast majority of occupations termed "high-status" and in all but a few advanced educational programs (Eccles, 1986; Reis, 1995). They receive many mixed messages about their abilities from their families and from the public and typically achieve less when compared to their male counterparts on standard measures valued by the culture.

Some have charged that females are denied opportunities, especially in traditional male domains, and that they underachieve. On the other hand, others have asserted that females are presented with a wider range of opportunity in life than males because they are accepted as homemakers, as well as professionals, whereas men are not (Rejskind, 1993). Impassioned discussion surrounds both assertions.

Actualization

Prompted by discussion of accomplishment in superior adult males 35 years after graduation from an Ivy League College (Gowan, 1972), the study described in this chapter was designed to examine a comparable group of 167 women ages 45–70 who resided in Martha Cook, an honors dormitory at the University of Michigan. One of the guiding questions is ripe for study today: What are the attributes that distinguish women who are actualized?

Initially, it was tempting to link creative accomplishment with career achievements only. After all, achievements in a field can be measured and analyzed quite quickly, and they can serve as a point of reference that others in the culture know. However, as Eccles (1986) argued, many women make contributions that are not considered "career achievements," but have profound and lasting impacts on the lives of many. To explain women's creative accomplishments solely in terms of achievement in traditional areas would be a mistake because it favors a stereotypically masculine perspective.

Dabrowski's Theory of Development

Several views of actualization, such as those of Maslow (1954) and Dabrowski (1964), encompass more than enculturated conceptions of achievement and include broader contexts of emotional, intellectual, and moral growth. Dabrowski's theory provided an elegant and applicable model from which data on Martha Cook women were analyzed. The theory consists of five levels of development, which are characterized as follows.

Level 1: Egocentric people are motivated by financial success, power, glory, and conquest. People at this level are motivated by winning. They are fierce competitors and often step on others to gain positions of leadership in competitive environments.

Level 2: Approval-seeking people are motivated by fear of disapproval or punishment from their social group. They are easily swayed by dominant and egocentric leaders.

Level 3: Those at this level experience emotional turmoil as they examine their own inadequacies. They understand who they could be and are dissatisfied with who they are.

Level 4:   Motivated by deep-rooted ideals, individuals at this level commit to responsibility and service to others. They have unshakable values and much integrity.

Level 5:   People at this level are motivated by the highest principles of love and compassion. Inner conflicts have been resolved, and they live in service to humanity.

Dabrowski (1964) was most interested in Levels 3, 4, and 5, where the human spirit transcends into advanced development and the individual begins to formulate an unshakable set of values. Inner conflict (Level 3) is necessary for the individual to move beyond group or cultural norms and is a necessary step in the process of actualization. Individuals at Level 4 integrate their "ideal self" with who they are and find ways to reach goals that benefit themselves and those around them. Those at Level 5 no longer struggle to integrate ideal values such as love, grace, compassion, and service into purpose-filled lives, but are committed to lives of altruism, service to others, harmonious relationships, authentic purpose, and empathy for all.

Different Forms of Actualization

There are stark contrasts between definitions of actualization that focus on competitive achievements and Dabrowski's definition (1964), which holds up "empathy and compassion for others" as moral exemplars. For example, Hollinger and Fleming (1992) defined actualization as "the achievement of societally valued and normatively defined 'high level/high status' educational and career goals commensurate with her talents and abilities" (p. 207), which ironically falls at the lowest levels according to Dabrowski's model. In practical terms, a woman with a "What's in it for me?" mentality who attains a position of power with little or no concern for others could be described as "actualized" according to Hollinger and Fleming. However, she would be described as "egocentric" and "brutally ambitious" by Dabrowski and would be placed at the lowest levels of human development until she learned to examine her own behavior, reflect upon her choices, and consider the effects of her choices on others. Gender equity research seems to vacillate between, on the one hand, wanting girls to earn titles, get ahead, and achieve in competitive arenas, and, on the other hand, actualize themselves through a deepening of personality and strengthening of moral conviction and spirit.

Recently, Silverman (1993, 1994) renewed attention to Dabrowski's theory and to inner components of actualization, especially emotion and moral sensitivity. She argued that protection of these sensitivities is critical to actualization of the self:

> The natural trajectory of giftedness in childhood is not a six-figure salary, perfect happiness, and a guaranteed place in *Who's Who*. It is the deepening of the personality, the strengthening of one's value system, the creation of greater and greater challenges for oneself, and the development of broader avenues for expressing compassion. Advanced development in adulthood is the commitment to becoming a better person and helping to make this a better world. (1994, p. 22)

Using Dabrowski's model of development (1964), the words and life decisions of the women of Martha Cook were studied. Specifically, attributes that characterized the most actualized MC women were examined here.

The Women of Martha Cook

We chose a group of 312 alumnae of the Martha Cook (MC) dormitory at the University of Michigan who were residents between 1950 and 1970. The group ranged in age from 45 to 70, with nearly half (48%) of the group about 50 years old. The women had the highest grade-point averages on campus; 80% were honor and scholarship award winners. Even the least academic women at MC scored in the top 10% on measures of potential and achievement. The women of MC were expected to lead campus organizations, abide by the honor code of behavior for MC, and donate their talents to the common good of both the dormitory and the university.

Quantitative and qualitative methods were used for this study. Data were collected using the Survey of University Women, which focused on family background, education, occupation, development of talent, and life satisfaction; articles, chapters, diaries, and recordings of their work; and other materials written about the women of MC. Survey items asked women to rank their priorities in life and to describe their most significant life events, accomplishments, and satisfactions.

A total of 167 surveys were completed and returned, providing a 54% response rate. (A random sample of nonresponders revealed that they were a very similar group to those who responded to the survey.) Two researchers read each completed survey, which was no small task given that many surveys included attached biographies, newspaper clippings, autobiographies, announcements of upcoming publications and performances, brochures, syllabi, vitae, publications and cassettes, letters, and articles and essays written by and about the MC women. We were also the audience for a number of women who gave detailed descriptions of pet peeves, unabashed love for husbands and families, spiritual growth, and views on local issues, abortion, current candidates, the President's initiatives, and so on. (It was naïve of the researchers to think that this creative group would simply respond to the survey; however, realization of this naivete came after the elaborate and creative responses were received.)

Responses to questions about "the most significant accomplishments in their lives" were analyzed using statistical procedures (ANOVA and chi-square) and constant comparison methods outlined by Strauss and Corbin (1990). Criteria for determining actualized MC women were based on Dabrowski's model and described by Hall and Hansen (1997).

What the Women of Martha Cook Revealed

The following eight characteristics describe the lives of the most actualized MC women.

1. **The actualized MC women were impelled by potent and personal life purposes.**

Their purposes were like "callings," and their need to act on those callings surpassed many of their other needs, specifically the need for approval from others and the need for financial security. The actualized MC women had deep personal insights and felt there were deep purposes to most of life's activities. They deliberately placed themselves in positions to achieve their purposes, as can be seen in the following comments:

> To major in English was inevitable; the call of stories had been a siren song ever since childhood. To delight readers with my words was the most exciting life I could imagine. Together (with my husband) we encouraged the children to use their time and talents to enrich their lives and make this world a better place in which to live.

> [The most significant event in the last 20 years was] becoming director of the nonprofit contemporary visual arts gallery where I . . . saw the gallery evolve into a widely respected cultural center in our community and beyond. The gallery is noted for its elegant and varied presentations, as well as for its responsibility in its dealing with artists.

Dabrowski (1964) distinguished between actualized individuals with personal purpose and insecure individuals who need others to validate their self-worth. Some MC women were hindered by their need for approval or financial security, as can be seen in these comments:

> I'm too concerned about what people will think of me. Too afraid of making mistakes; keeps me stuck in my job and prevents me from exploring my artistic potential.

> [My most significant accomplishment is that I] worked 20 years for the same boss.

A strong sense of purpose was noted by other researchers of gifted and eminent women and was described by Kerr (1985) as a powerful sense of personal mission and identity. Many of the

MC women felt a sense of personal mission and had progressed into Levels 4 and 5 of Dabrowski's model.

2. The actualized MC women valued relationships over professional achievements.

When asked to "describe the most meaningful event" they had experienced in the last 20 years, 83% of the MC women referred to a relationship-oriented event (birth, marriage, death, spiritual awakening), with the majority (52%) directly stating "raising my children." These were not women who chose "raising children" because they had little else to do. These were the same women who headed medical facilities, traveled the world, and wrote influential articles and books, to name a few worthy endeavors. In spite of fierce competition from other activities, the MC women chose "raising children" as the most meaningful life event.

Other research tells us that gifted women often place relationships at a premium. White (1990) followed up on students of the Speyer School (Hollingworth, 1926) and found that females claimed their children as their major accomplishment. Similarly, Post-Kammer and Perrone (1983) found that 73% of women studied reported that work was second in importance to close relationships.

Authentic empathy for others emerges during Level 4 of Dabrowski's model and translates into genuine empathy for one's family, friends, colleagues, and the world, both locally and globally. The MC women confirmed through their own words that human relationships were central in their lives and provided one of the foundations for their work.

3. The actualized MC women were committed to the common good.

One of the most powerful findings from this study was that the majority of MC women were service-oriented and committed to a common good. This makes sense given that they were selected to live in Martha Cook, in part, based on their willingness to contribute to the common good of the dormitory. Following college, the women served through their professions, their volunteer work, and their families and friends. They sensed an unselfish purpose for themselves and held close to a philosophy of servanthood that undergirded many aspects of their lives. The altruistic nature of the group as a whole pervaded the study, as can be seen in the following comment:

> Getting to a point in my career where I can see that my role is that of leadership and service and they are one and the same has given me a satisfying sense of accomplishment about the work that I've been involved with over much of the past 20 years.

While few of the MC women seemed selfish, those who pursued a sense of self solely through their family relationships or solely through achievement recognition were clearly distinguished from those who pursued paths leading to a common good. One woman, for example, stated, "I receive my self-esteem through the way my husband and family are perceived by our community."

Dabrowski (1964) characterized the highest levels of actualized persons (Level 5) by their altruism. Living a life in service to humanity is to live according to the highest standards of life. The most actualized MC women displayed qualities of altruism and service.

4. The actualized MC women led productive lives.

Another main finding emerging from the thematic analyses was that many of the MC women led extremely productive lives. According to their own words, they shared interests such as a happy home life, well-adjusted children, good friends, personal growth, and meaningful pursuits. The MC women's dual commitment to family and personal purpose is revealed in the following comment:

> My husband encouraged me to use my education, to acquire more when needed, just as I encouraged him to use his, to acquire a Ph.D. when he so desired. I feel we worked together to achieve this and, at the same time, to raise a large family.

In addition to working hard to develop the character of their families, the actualized MC women worked hard toward their personal purpose. Just listing their accomplishments would take a volume in and of itself. Briefly, MC women served as judges, conducted in world-famous music halls, administered well-known medical facilities, earned Fulbright scholarships, authored famous publications, were deans at well-known universities, were CEOs and company presidents, were listed in *Who's Who*, and were honored by the President of the United States and other dignitaries. One PTO worker in the study advocated for desegregation of Chicago public schools, another woman brought media to areas of the world for the first time, another hosted conferences in remote areas of the world, and others served as Peace Corps volunteers, explored exotic jungles, conducted archeological digs, volunteered to direct orchestras or choirs in local and world-class theaters, ministered to the needy through churches, mentored immigrants, and expressed their creativity through arts, theater groups, and beautification projects.

In contrast, other MC women struggled to be productive as can be seen in this comment: "My husband supports my endeavors financially as long as they don't interfere with what he sees as his need for attention from me. I have no other source of income."

Productive MC women had reached at least Level 4 of Dabrowski's model, the level where individuals have found a way to reach their own ideals. People at Level 4 are generally effective leaders who show high degrees of responsibility, effectiveness, objectivity, and productivity along lines that benefit others in society.

5. The actualized MC women were profoundly optimistic.

The MC women were like all other women in that they lived through life's intermittent turmoil, upheaval, and emotional uncertainty. However, some MC women maintained a sort of equilibrium through it all. They were able to withstand intense decentering experiences and the accompanying pain and confusion. The turmoil helped them recenter, cope, and strengthen their optimism, as can be seen in the following comments:

> At age 27, I divorced my husband of 5 years and with-
> out alimony or child support . . . raised three children.
> I worked continuously, and though I married again at
> age 50, my husband died 9 weeks later. As a result of
> my husband's death, I retired alone. This stage of my
> life . . . is totally unlike the early part. However, I build
> on those past experiences and they make this such a
> delicious period.

I definitely believe that good things are always happening. That
phrase was the beginning theme for my essay in 1963 when I
sought entrance to the Martha Cook Building. I still believe it.
And, 30 years later, I have lots of accumulated experience to further prove that thesis.

> Knowing that I have a great number of diverse inner
> resources that are available in difficult times and that I
> have the ability to turn most any circumstance in posi-
> tive directions is very empowering.

The researchers were amazed at the levels of optimism
revealed by the actualized MC women. It was not because their
lives were easier that they were more optimistic; rather, it was
because they chose to see the good that happened in their lives.
At higher levels of Dabrowski's model, the choice to grow is conscious. Actualized people recognize that pain is inevitable if one
is to grow, and they hold a life perspective that allows them to
translate painful experiences into growth steps. Their perspective allows them to "count their blessings" in the darkest hours
of their lives and enables them to move forward with strength,
resolve, and hope.

6. The actualized MC women worked for balance in their lives.

Nearly all the MC women worked for balance in their lives.
They feared gypping those who relied on them personally
(mostly spouses and children) and did not want to sacrifice personal relationships in order to heed their calling. At the same
time, though, they did not want to sacrifice their calling solely

for personal relationships. They admitted to struggling with issues of balance in their lives and tried not to take the well-being of themselves, their families, or their friends for granted, as can be seen in this representative comment:

> My life is most satisfying when I am able to balance my family, my friends, my church, my job, and my recreational activities. I must confess this is not always easy to do. But, when it all comes together, it is exciting and rewarding.

Those who recognized the importance of "love and work" in their lives were distinguished from their counterparts who compromised on close relationships in order to pursue achievement goals or those who compromised on their calling in order to preserve a close relationship, generally with their spouse. The actualized women were supported by relationships that were characterized by interdependence and served to bring out the best in them and those they cared about. Because they balanced their need to create and their need for relationships, they were not faced with the psychosocial dilemma of choosing between standards of achievement and attainment of intimacy (Gross, 1989). In general, their families enjoyed their intellectual drive and commitment to service, and they were not asked to choose between meaningful family relationships and a meaningful path of growth. They had both.

Dabrowski (1964) stressed a dual commitment to human relationships and to moral purpose. In fact, deep moral purpose at the higher levels of his model was not possible without meaningful relationships, According to Dabrowski, one must have both to be actualized.

7. The actualized MC women were morally sensitive.

Actualized MC women were characterized by their deep and powerful moral sensitivity. It is an understatement to describe such awareness of the needs of others—be they physical, intellectual, spiritual, or emotional—as "inspiring." This selected comment from an MC woman is just one example of the deep moral sensitivity witnessed in so many of the other MC women.

> After 4 months of work, and . . . in light of a lot of devastating information about how the Vietnamese people felt about losing their orphaned children, we made an agonizing decision not to be a part of an adoption from Vietnam. Miraculously, 2 months later, our local social worker found us a beautiful 4-month-old Caucasian boy whom we adopted.

One cannot transcend the lower levels of actualization, according to Dabrowski (1964), without keen moral insight. To couple a personal life purpose that betters the world with a commitment to growing relationships and service to others requires moral sensitivity. Actualized people, according to Dabrowski, not only have moral sensitivity, but exercise that sensitivity in order to notice and meet the often undetected needs of others.

8. The actualized MC women revealed a mature personal life perspective.

As a group, the actualized MC women commonly offered a perspective on life that included sickness, death, and loss, as well as accomplishments and achievements—the good and the bad. Many women described changed priorities prompted by pivotal life events that put their view of life in a different light, such as losing a spouse or child or having medical or emotional problems. While many women experience dramatic life events, actualized women reflect upon the lessons learned from these traumatic crises and put such defining times into a positive life perspective. For example, one woman said,

> The death of my 30-year-old daughter [was my most meaningful life event]. She was a wonderful person, respected and liked by many. She was a lawyer and was diagnosed with multiple sclerosis in 1989. I'm sorry she had that terrible illness, but am glad she could share it with many friends and colleagues so they could benefit from an understanding of her life and death.

The ability to look at oneself and one's life objectively and compassionately is necessary to be actualized according to

Dabrowski (1964), and there is little doubt that many of the MC women did just that. Their rich inner life and resulting life perspective allowed them a solid place in a world with slippery values. Their perspective provided meaning for them personally and provided a sense of inner peace and satisfaction with life.

Conclusion

For the most part, the actualized MC women remained emotionally available to their family and friends, and they talked openly about trusted relationships while consistently forwarding their life's purpose. They were not willing to set aside their contributions to society. They owned their own sense of purpose in life and did not sublimate their own goals for the goals of their spouse, children, or others. Their altruism came through their careers and volunteer accomplishments at the same time they enhanced the lives of others. Through their inner strength and optimism, they were able to overcome many of life's disappointments and challenges. They expected support from their spouse and family and attempted to be interdependent, rather than dependent. They actualized their talents and were able to contribute to society in the process.

The eight characteristics that described the lives of the most actualized MC women can and should be shared with gifted girls as they make their way through the school years. Teacher and counselors can use the lessons learned by these exceptional women to support today's gifted girls and inspire them to reach for success in all endeavors in their lives. These lesson can show gifted girls that, if a woman values her personal mission, as well as unity with family and others, she is more likely to seek her own steadfast growth in both areas. She will look for opportunities that will serve her personal mission and relationships with others.

References

Dabrowski, K. (1964). *Positive disintegration*. London: Little, Brown.

Eccles, J. S. (1986). Gender roles and women's achievement-related decisions. *Educational Researcher, 15*(6), 15–19.

Gowan, J. C. (1972). Levels of development and accomplishment in superior male adults. In J. C. Gowan (Ed.), *The guidance and measurement of intelligence, development, and creativity* (pp. 205–217). Northridge: California State University.

Gross, M. U. M. (1989). The pursuit of excellence or the search for intimacy? The forced choice dilemma of gifted youth. *Roeper Review, 11,* 189–194.

Hall, E. G., & Hansen, J. B. (1997). Self-actualizing men and women: A comparison study. *Roeper Review, 20,* 22–27.

Hollinger, C. L., & Fleming, E. S. (1992). A longitudinal examination of life choices of gifted and talented young women. *Gifted Child Quarterly, 36,* 207–212.

Hollingworth, L. S. (1926). *Gifted children: Their nature and nurture.* New York: MacMillian.

Kerr, B. (1985). *Smart girls, gifted women.* Columbus: Ohio Psychology Press.

Maslow, A. (1954). *Motivation and personality.* New York: Harper.

Post-Kammer, P., & Perrone, P. (1983). Career perceptions of talented individuals: A follow-up study. *Vocational Guidance Quarterly, 31,* 203–211.

Reis, S. (1995). Talent ignored, talent diverted: The cultural context underlying giftedness in females. *Gifted Child Quarterly, 39,* 162–170.

Rejskind, G. (1993, November). *Boys and girls together: Toward gender equity in education.* Paper presented at the annual meeting of the National Association for Gifted Children, Atlanta, GA.

Silverman, L. K. (Ed.). (1993). *Counseling the gifted and talented.* Denver: Love.

Silverman, L. K. (1994). The moral sensitivity of gifted children and the evolution of society. *Roeper Review, 17,* 110–115.

Strauss, A., & Corbin, J. (1990). *Basics of qualitative research: Grounded theory procedures and techniques.* Thousand Oaks, CA: Sage.

White, W. L. (1990). Interviews with child I, child J, and child L. *Roeper Review, 12,* 222–227.

chapter 9

Helping Teachers to Encourage Talented Girls in Mathematics

by **M. Katherine Gavin** *and* **Sally M. Reis**

*j*ennifer was an A student, not just in mathematics, but in all of her subjects. She was in an accelerated seventh-grade algebra class—the only accelerated class in her suburban middle school. Mathematics had been easy for Jennifer in elementary school. She paid attention in class, did her homework, and excelled in facts and algorithms, but now she was in a class with all of the highest achieving students in her grade, and new concepts were being presented in challenging ways. She could no longer rely upon her memory to complete her assignments and was experiencing confusion and frustration if she did not instantly know the answer or understand the method to solve problems. Meanwhile, other students, especially some of the boys, seemed to call out answers faster and were able to answer the challenging questions posed by the teacher. Jennifer believed that she needed more time to think about these questions. She wasn't getting that time in her class, and her anxiety about math grew.

Jennifer isn't alone. Young gifted females may not receive necessary encouragement to achieve in mathematics. An American Association of University Women (AAUW) report (Wellesley College Center for Research on Women, 1992) concluded that "all differences in math performance between girls and boys at ages 11 and 15 could be accounted for by differences among those scoring in the top 10–20%" (p. 25). This means that many of our brightest female mathematics students are not keeping up with their male counterparts. It is clear from this and other research studies discussed in this chapter that many mathematically talented females perform at levels that are not commensurate with their abilities (Reis, 1987; Reis & Callahan, 1989).

However, the situation can be improved, for teachers and parents can implement specific strategies to help talented girls succeed in math.

Jennifer, for example, is at a critical point in her mathematical development. While she wants to please her parents and teachers by excelling in algebra, she is becoming increasingly anxious about mathematics and is afraid she may no longer make the honor roll because of her grades in math. She spends more time on homework, yet she receives fewer A's than before. Therefore, she needs encouragement from her parents to assure her that B grades are acceptable in accelerated courses. She needs support from her teachers to encourage her to use the time she needs to really think about concepts and to formulate her own foundations of mathematical thinking. She also needs to know that everyone, even mathematicians, experience similar states of discomfort when they encounter challenging content. In fact, mathematical insights and future discoveries often emerge from confusion. If Jennifer is to be successful and remain in this class, her teacher should provide a classroom environment that will help her develop her mathematical abilities and regain her confidence regarding her ability to do advanced work. This environment should nurture creative thinking and encourage risk taking, as well as use alternative assessments, such as mathematics portfolios and creative projects. Jennifer's teachers can also serve as sources of support who will encourage her strengths and help her overcome her decreasing self-confidence.

Stereotyping About Females and Mathematics

Before we can alleviate the problems experienced by girls like Jennifer, it is important to try to understand the factors behind those problems. One of the main reasons that girls do not succeed in mathematics may not be due to any lack of ability or effort; rather, it may attributed to the fact that they are not *expected* to excel in this area by some of their parents, teachers, or peers.

Stereotypes influence perceptions and performance in school and in life and are often cited as contributing to girls' problems in math and related fields such as technology. Unfortunately, mathematics is often thought of as a "male" field, and our society holds traditional male images of scientists, engineers, computer scientists, and mathematicians. Society's influence is also demonstrated in the development of software for student use. Software continues to be geared toward male interests, with males being the heroes in 63% of the software examined in one study (Nelson & Watson, 1991). Not only is there a need for software in which girls will have an interest, but also girls' interests need to be expanded so that gender-based stereotypes are not reinforced (Sanders, 1994).

Evidence also exists that girls are regarded as less capable in mathematics by some of their teachers and parents, and these perceptions may influence girls' opinions of their own abilities. For example, Kissane (1986) found that teachers were less accurate in nominating girls who are likely to do well on the quantitative subtest of the SAT than they were in naming boys who were likely to score high. Siegle and Reis (1994) found that adolescent female gifted students indicated that they had higher abilities than males in language arts only, while male gifted students indicated they had higher abilities than females in mathematics, science, and social studies.

It is important to examine beliefs because they influence actions. For example, current data indicate that, of the 11,793 students who took the AP Computer Science A exam, only 1,959 (17%) were female. On the more extensive or more difficult AP Computer Science AB exam taken by 6,450 students, only 611 (9%) were female. Men comprised the vast majority of test takers, as 91% of those taking either test were male.

Looking at the implications of this at the local level, Henry and Manning (1998) reported that only one girl enrolled in the math class entitled "Introduction to Computer" at a particular high school during the 1998 academic year, and no girls were enrolled in "Advanced Computer."

Mathematics Grades in School

In her review of the literature on women's mathematics achievement, Kimball (1989) found that, while standardized test scores still favor boys, grade differences favor girls. The pattern of performance on standardized aptitude assessment measures is also very different from the pattern of grades. While males' mean scores on both the verbal and math sections of the 1996 SAT were higher than females', the females who took the test had a higher mean high school grade-point average: 3.27 overall, versus 3.11 for males (Educational Testing Service, 1996).

How does this affect gifted females in particular? Rosser (1989) reported that the higher the grades, the greater the gender gap: "Girls with an A+ grade point average averaged 23 points lower on the SAT-Verbal section (9 points lower than the overall verbal M/F gap) and 60 points lower on the SAT-Mathematics section than boys with the same GPA" (p. iv). Also, we cannot discount the influence of societal expectations and the media discussion of SAT scores on the confidence level of females as they enter the classroom to take the exam. Do they have a mindset that they will not do well on these tests? If so, how much does this affect their performance? This is worthy of further examination.

Kimball (1989) made a fascinating point about the ways that we currently measure mathematics achievement: "Although there is ample evidence of young women's superior math achievement when grades are used to measure achievement, they have not been considered seriously in the literature on mathematics achievement. I am proposing that it is important to begin to take them seriously" (p. 203). Kimball suggested that classroom grades reflect what is learned during a particular class and should not be influenced by other experiences outside of, or prior to, the classroom experience. Also, the information that girls are not at a disadvantage and, in fact, have a grade advantage in many courses may be useful in increasing girls' confidence in their mathematics ability.

Postsecondary and Career Choices

Many gifted females continue to reject mathematics and directly related fields such as computer science and engineering as courses of study. Using data from the National Education Longitudinal Study of 1988 (NELS:88), a 10-year data collection project sponsored by the U.S. Government, Gavin (1997) examined a cohort of approximately 1,400 high-mathematics-ability students. As seniors in 1992, these students were surveyed to determine their intended fields of study in college. Although all students had been identified as having high mathematics ability, only 27% expressed interest in a mathematics or science major, with only 1.8% intending to major in mathematics. The numbers for females were quite revealing: only 9 (0.7%) selected computer science, 46 (3.3%) engineering, 19 (1.4%) mathematics, and 27 (2%) physical science. Examining data on intended majors for females who took the SAT in 1996, of those intending to major in engineering, only 19% were female, and in computer or information sciences, just 25% (Educational Testing Service, 1996). These remarkably low percentages of career interest in mathematics and science occur despite data cited earlier suggesting that females receive consistently higher grades in elementary school, secondary school, and in college-related subjects.

Although much attention has been given to research studies that have reported equal numbers of males and females declaring mathematics as their major field of study, it is important to study those who actually graduate with a mathematics major and pursue a mathematics career. While equal numbers of males and females start with the mathematics major, females comprise 43% of those completing the undergraduate major and only 20% of those completing the doctoral degree (Linn & Kessel, 1995). With respect to females who are minorities, the numbers are extremely low. Of the 1,209 mathematics Ph.D. degrees awarded in 1995–96, only 2 were went to Black women and 1 was earned by a Hispanic female (National Science Foundation,

1996). In terms of related fields, an examination of the distribution of the Ph.D. degrees awarded in 1992 revealed that women were awarded 16% of the degrees in computer science, 11% of the degrees in physics, and 8% of the engineering degrees (National Science Foundation, 1992). And, while the number of women in the life sciences fields has grown steadily since the early 1970s, the participation of women in physics and engineering reached a plateau at about 15% and has remained at this level for the past decade (Campbell, 1996). In fact, although women presently comprise 43% of the workforce, they make up only 10% of all engineers and 28% of mathematical and computer scientists (U.S. Census Bureau, 1999). Especially alarming is the high-paying area of technology, where men dominate the field, making up 70% of the high-tech labor force. The percentage of female computer professionals has actually decreased from 35.4 to 29.1% in the 1990s (U.S. Bureau of Labor Statistics, 1999).

Using Specific Strategies to Help Talented Girls in Mathematics

In today's technologically driven society, the need for workers in fields requiring mathematics and science backgrounds is constantly increasing. We must encourage more females to enter the field of mathematics. We have failed in our efforts to do this in the past. Research has consistently demonstrated the critical role of teachers in encouraging girls in mathematics. For example, Leroux and Ho (1994), in a qualitative study of 15 gifted female high school students , concluded:

> Female math teachers who act as role models are significant influences. Teachers who treat both genders equally, provide a warm, uninhibiting environment, and are approachable seem to provide the most 'psychologically safe' environment that is conducive to girls learning. (p. 45)

Demonstrating the kinds of effects that teachers can have on students, Rogers (1990), in a study of high-ability students, found that significant success in attracting females to higher level mathematics courses was achieved by teachers, either male or female, who created a classroom environment open and supportive of all students, one in which the teacher's style was conducive to the nature of mathematical inquiry. Gavin (1996) found that almost half of the female mathematics majors at a competitive college attributed their decision to major in mathematics to the influence of a high school teacher. In fact, one third of the students developed and maintained a personal relationship with these teachers throughout their college years. Confirming this at the graduate level, Becker (1994) conducted in-depth interviews with 31 graduate students and found that a successful teacher was frequently described as one who piqued students' interests by providing an enriched curriculum. She concluded that teachers and instruction could make a difference in all students' career choices.

The following strategies have been suggested by experts and shown to be effective in encouraging young girls in mathematics (Campbell 1992; Hanson, 1992). They can be implemented fairly easily and quickly.

1. *Teachers should consider their own feelings about mathematics and how these feelings might affect their teaching and students.* If a teacher does not like mathematics, has ambivalent feelings toward the subject, or a genuine fear of it, he or she may inadvertently be transferring some of these feelings to students. Fear or dislike of math may clearly be reflected in preferences for the curriculum covered in the gifted program and in the types of materials in the program. Gifted programs at the elementary level often focus on language arts, which reflects the strength of the teacher. However, it is imperative that the focus be shifted from the teacher to the student. The strengths and interests of the students should be identified and nurtured in gifted programs, and teachers must seek out resources to develop appropriate programs.

2. *Assume personal responsibility to encourage talented females in mathematics.* Adolescent girls who are talented in mathematics may receive mixed messages from parents, their peer group, and society in general. They need specific support to help them believe that they are truly talented in mathematics

and to encourage them to continue to pursue these areas in high school, college, and beyond.

Teachers who try to encourage talented girls may believe that they should help their students solve problems. However, strategies such as giving extra help may be detrimental to females' sense of self-confidence. Rather, teachers should encourage students to persist in seeking their own solutions. For example, they should answer questions with a question, giving hints, but not solutions. They must have high expectations for girls, let them know it, and praise them for being able to solve challenging problems.

Teachers must also be aware that females who are talented in mathematics are often talented in other academic areas, as well. Without encouragement to pursue their talent in these areas, they often choose other more female-oriented fields. Teachers must make parents aware of the need to support their daughters' talents in mathematics. In school, older girls taking Advanced Placement courses can be asked to come and talk to younger students to encourage them to participate in these courses. At every stage, all opportunities should remain available to talented female students. They should be encouraged to enroll in and complete advanced mathematics and computer classes.

3. *Create a safe, caring, and supportive learning environment.* Eccles (1987) drew several conclusions from the existing literature about mathematics and science teachers who have been successful in reversing stereotypes and keeping females interested in mathematics. She noted a pattern of conditions in these classrooms, including:

- frequent use of cooperative learning opportunities,
- frequent individualized learning opportunities,
- use of practical problems in assignments,
- frequent use of hands-on opportunities,
- active career and educational guidance,
- infrequent use of competitive motivational strategies,
- frequent activities oriented toward broadening views of mathematics and physical sciences,
- presenting mathematics as a tool in solving problems, and
- frequent use of strategies to ensure full class participation.

It is important to point out the similarity of these curricular and instructional practices to those recommended by the National Council of Teachers of Mathematics (2000) in their Principles and Standards for School Mathematics. In fact, these are the kinds of practices touted by the leaders in mathematics education as being essential for all students.

We translate these research findings into practical ideas for the classroom with the following suggestions. All girls, especially adolescents, need classrooms in which they will be heard and understood and where they can discuss ideas before coming to conclusions. The teacher should provide a setting where students are not permitted to call out answers randomly and where there is plenty of think time—periods of uncontested silence that may encourage students to become more willing to share their thinking with others. Teachers should not rush to provide closure to a lesson, for a mulling period is often essential for talented girls studying advanced topics. An effective strategy is the think-pair-share technique in which, after time for private thought, students share their answers with a neighbor and then with the entire class. The paired discussion lends credibility to their thinking, fosters mathematical communication, and develops a sense of confidence.

Teachers should also become personally aware of the additional attention they sometimes give to boys. It is hard to deny a waving hand or someone calling out, but increased attention, even negative attention, can reinforce behaviors. Girls need equal attention, and, to ensure that teachers provide it, peer observations can be established with colleagues. Using this technique, a teacher observes a peer's class and tallies the number of times girls and boys are called on. One way that some teachers address the issue of classroom equality is simply to alternate between calling on males and females in class.

Some current research indicates that girls tend to thrive in small-group work, especially all-female groups. In coed groups, boys may dominate, becoming the leaders and monopolizing the discussion, while girls become the recorders of the discussion. This is especially true in computer work. Boys have been found to monopolize computers even in preschool (Nelson & Watson, 1991). When boys and girls are paired together at the computer, research has found that a girl will defer to her partner's wishes

(Martin & Murchie-Beyma, 1992; Volman, 1997). Current research indicates that, by the third or fourth grade, girls are less technologically oriented (Nelson & Watson). Boys are at least three times more likely than girls to be involved with computers during the secondary and postsecondary years (Kramer & Lehman, 1990). Thus, it is important that girls be given the opportunity to work individually on computers or, when working in pairs, be given a decision-making role and time for hands-on computer use.

Opportunities for students to reflect in writing about their ideas and fears about mathematics can also be provided in a safe and supportive class. A comment box enables students to drop a note about their feelings or their understanding of the content of the daily mathematics lesson, including questions they have and related topics they would like to pursue. E-mail also provides the opportunity for students to contact the teacher with questions or concerns.

Feelings can also be addressed in creative journal assignments, including mathematics metaphors as suggested by Buerk and Gibson (1994). A sample assignment might be the following: "If mathematics were a food (color, animal, etc.), it would be . . . and why?" The results can quickly foster communication and provide information about personal feelings. Journals can also be used to encourage communication about mathematical concepts and offer talented students a way to bring deeper understanding and new insight to areas they wish to pursue. Girls may often enjoy the intimate student-teacher dialogue created by the journal-writing process. An outgrowth of this experience could be the creation of discussion groups at lunch or after-school clubs in which girls can discuss their feelings and explore interesting mathematics topics.

4. *Provide some single-sex learning opportunities in mathematics.* There has been a renewed interest in single sex schools and classes for girls, although the research results on the effects of the single-sex environment have been quite contradictory, leaving one with what Gill (1996) referred to as "a now-you-see-it-now-you-don't effect that is both tantalizing and frustrating." However, researchers agree that there seems to be a qualitative difference in the single-sex class environment that makes many girls prefer it to a coed classroom.

In her studies of middle school girls, Streitmatter (1997) found that girls were more likely to ask and answer questions in single-sex math classrooms and that the girls-only setting enhanced their ability to learn and was overwhelmingly preferred. The single-sex setting seems especially useful in mathematics, where females' self-esteem is traditionally lower. All girls' math classes are being experimented with throughout the United States. Although some districts have been concerned with legal ramifications, other districts have found that, if all-boys classes are also offered or if boys are given the opportunity to take the classes designed for girls (few want this option), then this does not present a problem. In fact, Gavin and Shmurak (1999) found that, in an urban middle school setting, the boys in single-sex classes benefited the most by making significant gains on state mathematics mastery test scores when compared with their counterparts in coed classes.

Math clubs for girls, computer camps for girls, and summer math programs for girls such as SummerMath at Mount Holyoke College are all empowering ways for females to explore mathematics in nonthreatening environments. Some girls, especially at the upper elementary and middle school levels, feel intimidated by the male dominance in competitive math leagues such as Math Olympiad and MathCounts; yet, these leagues provide talented students with challenging mathematical problems and a forum for teachers and peers to recognize mathematical talent. Some teachers have created all-female Math Olympiad and MathCounts teams that have worked well (Volpe, 1999). Establishing clubs for girls as after-school or activity-period alternatives also gives girls the freedom to confront math anxiety, if it exists, and to delve into complex problems in a friendly environment (Karp & Niemi, 2000). Female role models in various math-related professions can be guest speakers at the club meetings, and field trips taken to explore career options may inspire a budding mathematician.

A word of caution is necessary. It is important to remember that it is the nurturing environment provided by the teacher that makes these single-sex settings work. An AAUW roundtable of experts concluded that a single-sex classroom with a sexist teacher is just as detrimental as a coed classroom with the same type of teacher (Wellesley College Center for Research on Women, 1998).

5. *Appeal to the strengths of females as motivators.* During middle school and usually continuing through their adolescent years, mathematically talented females exhibit great attention to detail in their work, strong organizational skills, and, for some, a sophisticated level of maturity. These skills can be used to motivate girls' interest in mathematics.

One way to do this is by encouraging them to organize a Family Math Night (EQUALS, 1989) at the elementary school for parents and children to engage in fun mathematics activities. The girls choose activities for the evening, issue invitations, and set up and actually run the entire event (under the auspices of a teacher-mentor). Tutoring younger children and organizing mathematics clubs or Saturday enrichment programs also encourages and empowers talented adolescent females.

Some research evidence indicates that classes emphasizing *competition* result in higher achievement for males and classrooms that encourage *cooperation* result in higher achievement for females (Peterson & Fennema, 1985). However, these results may not always apply to some females who are mathematically talented. In a qualitative study of female mathematics majors enrolled in a highly selective women's college, Gavin (1996) found that these young women had actually enjoyed competition in their high school classrooms, especially when it involved males. Similarly, when Hernandez Garduño (1997) investigated gifted females' and males' achievement and attitudes about advanced math, she found that talented girls liked fast-paced competitive classes and disliked cooperative learning situations that held them back.

The implications of these research results indicate that teachers need to recognize that all females are not alike and have different learning styles. They need to observe the females in their class and be especially aware of the needs of the talented females, some of whom may break the mold. They should provide some competitive, some cooperative, and some individual learning situations and allow choice whenever possible so as to maximize student interest and learning.

Other research indicates that boys like to experiment and tinker, while girls are more goal-oriented in school and feel that tinkering may be a waste of time (Martin & Murchie-Beyma, 1992). Because some girls have been socialized to play more often with dolls, rather than blocks, and to read books, rather than tinker with fixing their bicycles, they may need more time to work with manipulatives. They may also need in-class time to build models, to see how things work, and to develop their sense of spatial relationships.

The activity Cooperative Geometry (EQUALS, 1986) is another excellent example of group work with manipulatives that develops spatial thinking and encourages a true cooperative problem-solving spirit. The extensions are especially challenging for talented elementary and middle school students. Equally good for upper elementary and middle school students is the unit "Ruins of Montarek" from the new NSF-funded mathematics series, Connected Mathematics Program (Lappan, Fey, Fitzgerald, Friel, & Phillips, 1998). In this unit, Emily Hawkins, a famous explorer and adventurer, investigates the ancient ruins of the lost city of Montarek by making models of buildings from the clues found at the ruins. Another investigation that features a female role model is an episode from the Jasper Woodbury series (Learning Technology Center, 1996) entitled "The Right Angle." In this episode, a young Native American female searches for a treasure left to her by her grandfather. Students work cooperatively using maps and compasses to locate the treasure.

6. *Use language, problems, and activities that are relevant to girls.* Damarin (1990) examined traditional mathematics vocabulary and found that it reflects a strong male influence. The language contains goals of *mastery* and mathematical *power*. We teach students to *attack* problems and our instructional strategies include *drill* and *competitions*. She believes that, instead of talking about working toward mastery, teachers should talk about *internalization* of concepts. Instead of attacking problems, students should be encouraged to *interact* with them, *sharing* problems, and working *cooperatively* toward solutions.

Rather than focusing mainly on activities relating to football yardage, baseball statistics, and housing construction, teachers should also consciously incorporate problems and activities that girls enjoy. Problems dealing with endangered species, recycling, the spread of disease, population growth, and quilting have proven to be excellent suggestions. Activities involving patterns such as tangrams, paper folding, and tessellations and those involving art such as making mobiles, origami, computer graphics, and scale drawings may also appeal to many girls. Some favorite teacher resource materials with activities to encourage girls in mathematics are listed in the appendix at the end of this book.

7. *Create a challenging curriculum.* Teachers must encourage talented females to seek challenging opportunities when studying mathematics. Moving students beyond the familiar with ideas that stretch the mind should be a major goal of a program for all talented students, including females. From elementary school exposure to such topics as different numeration systems, the Fibonacci Numbers, and nonroutine problem solving, to secondary school study of non-Euclidean geometry, fractals, chaos theory, and combinatorics, students need to struggle with a change of mindset and relish this struggle, for it fosters a deep, intimate, and broadened understanding of mathematics.

In designing curricula for talented females, teachers should include a variety of alternative assessments. As some talented females may not do their best thinking during timed tests, other options will enable them to demonstrate their knowledge and competencies. Independent and small-group projects provide an ideal medium to showcase talent. These projects should go beyond a typical term paper and should focus on investigative activities in which students assume the role of firsthand inquirers—thinking, feeling, and acting like practicing professionals. In the Enrichment Triad Model (Renzulli, 1977), student products are used as the vehicle to develop research skills and provide an opportunity to use authentic methodology. This is an excellent opportunity to entice girls to use technology as an effective tool for advanced research, especially in gathering and analyzing data.

The report *Tech Savvy: Educating Girls in the New Computer Age* (Wellesley College Center for Research on Women, 2000) makes it clear that the reason girls are not represented well in computer classes is that they are critical of the computer culture, rather than the mistaken belief that they are computer phobic. Using technology to support interesting, independent projects is one way for females to realize the usefulness of computers.

These projects are most effective when they are primarily directed toward bringing about a desired impact on an audience, whether it be fellow students, administrators, town officials, mathematicians, or senior citizens. The teacher functions as a facilitator, pointing the student in the direction of resource people and materials as needed or providing direction in learning methodology to conduct the investigation. Some examples of these projects might include contacting local community officials for needed surveying or design projects, such as a population survey or a statistical analysis on the use of current library facilities or an energy audit of the town hall using mathematical analysis with recommendations to the town council for improved efficiency. The National Council of Teachers of Mathematics addenda series book, *Data Analysis and Statistics Across the Curriculum, Grades 9–12* (1992), is an excellent resource for long and short-term projects with timelines and evaluation criteria.

With the increased use of block scheduling at the middle and high school level, another means for offering challenging and interesting mathematics to students is the use of enrichment clusters. Enrichment clusters are groups of students who share common interests and who come together during designated time blocks to pursue these interests (Renzulli, 1994). Single-sex enrichment groups can provide an increased sense of confidence for females. During these extended time periods, students can pursue mutual mathematical interests together. For example, they might study fractals using computer models and decide to create programs that generate original fractal pieces. Or, they might gather to start a Young Architects' Guild focusing on learning about architectural design. Using this knowledge, they may decide to create a play space for children at a local preschool or redesign a veterinarian's office space for more efficient use. Again, the teacher acts as a guide and the students are empowered to discover math and see its relevance in the real world. They learn to value mathematics and, hopefully, become inspired to continue study and pursue a mathematically related career.

8. *Provide female role models and mentors.* Many teachers understand that some girls have unique ways of connecting to people. Teachers should capitalize on this and include an histor-

ical perspective in their mathematics curriculum to help students become aware of both the people and the creative processes behind mathematics. The lives of mathematicians, their interests in the subject, and how they created their mathematical discoveries will help young female students to appreciate the creative process, as well as the difficulties faced in getting new theories accepted. It is interesting to discover that concepts as basic as the notion of zero, irrational numbers, and negative numbers were quite controversial when first presented and were adopted only with great difficulty.

The names of the female mathematicians—Hypatia, Marie Agnesi, Sophie Germain, Evelyn Boyd Granville, Sonya Kovalevskaya, Mary Somerville—are usually not recognized by boys or girls. Teachers can make these women come alive by celebrating their birthdays, hanging their portraits in bulletin board displays, and encouraging females to perform autobiographical skits dressed in their period costumes. Videotaped interviews conducted between student reporters and a remarkable woman who has suddenly come back to life in the 21st century can also be effective. This provides a creative twist to the historical perspective that appeals to some talented females.

Role models need not all be historical; examples of women currently working in mathematics and related fields—Ph.D. mathematicians, computer scientists, astronauts, engineers, physicists, astronomers, and so on—can be presented, as well. The Internet is an exciting medium for students that allows them to enter into dialogue with these professionals. (Some excellent resources on the lives of female mathematicians, with interesting anecdotal family and personal stories, are included in the Appendix at the end of the book.)

A rewarding experience for teachers, as well as girls, is organizing and participating in a career day in mathematics, science, and technology. At these conferences, which are generally held for girls in middle or high school, female professionals conduct hands-on workshop sessions with girls, interacting with them and exposing them to actual on-the-job activities that spark career interest in girls. It is exciting and rewarding to visit these sessions and observe girls listening to a dog's heartbeat with a veterinarian, performing a chemical test on local river water with an environmental engineer, or trying to determine car insurance rates for teenage girls with an actuary. An association that can assist teachers in planning these days is Expanding Your Horizons, Math-Science Network located at 2727 College Ave., Berkeley, CA 94705.

We have conducted several of these career days at the University of Connecticut and found that, in addition to the hands-on workshops, panels of professional women are also effective and allow a greater variety of careers to be represented. To enliven these panels and encourage interaction between the women and the often shy female students, we highly recommend using the "Tool Clues" activity designed by EQUALS with the address listed in the appendix. In this activity, female professionals provide bags of "tools" used in their careers, and students, working in groups, try to guess their profession using a 20-question format.

One of the greatest benefits from these interactions with professional women is the opportunity for establishing mentorship and internship programs. Participating in these programs gives mathematically talented females the opportunity to work directly with a female role model in a high-level mathematics-related career position.

Conclusion

Far fewer females than males major in mathematics and pursue careers in mathematics and related fields. It is our responsibility to try to make high-tech, high paying professional careers equally available to all students. As pointed out in this chapter, few talented students of either sex indicate an interest in majoring in mathematics. The majority of the strategies we have suggested above are of the type recommended not only for girls, but also for all students by the National Council of Teachers of Mathematics (2000) in their Principles and Standards for School Mathematics. These strategies and activities focus on constructivist, discovery-oriented learning as the key to building mathematical confidence and understanding in all students.

So, in reality, promoting equality in the classroom is also promoting good teaching techniques, developing student problem-solving abilities, and instilling a genuine appreciation for mathematics. Only the wider use of these strategies will provide answers to questions about how we can continue to recruit the number of talented people we need into careers in mathematical areas in the future. What should be clear to all of us is that too few talented females regard a career involving mathematics as an attainable goal, and it is vitally important to encourage and support more females to pursue this area of study in the future.

References

Becker, J. R. (1994, April). *Research on gender and mathematics perspectives and new directions.* Paper presented at the annual meeting of the American Educational Research Association, New Orleans, LA.

Buerk, D., & Gibson, H. (1994). Students' metaphors for mathematics: Gathering, interpreting, implications. *WME Newsletter, 16*(2), 2–8.

Campbell, G. (1996). *National Action Council for Minorities in Engineering, Inc. research letter.* New York: National Action Council for Minorities in Engineering.

Campbell, P. B. (1992). *Nothing can stop us now: Designing effective programs for girls in math, science, and engineering.* Newton, MA: Women's Educational Equity Act.

Damarin, S. K. (1990). Teaching mathematics: A feminist perspective. In T. J. Cooney & C. R. Hirsch (Eds.), *Teaching and learning mathematics in the 1990's* (pp. 144–158). Reston, VA: National Council of Teachers of Mathematics.

Eccles, J. S. (1987). Gender roles and women's achievement-related decisions. *Psychology of Women Quarterly, 11,* 135–171.

Educational Testing Service. (1996). *1996 college-bound seniors: A profile of SAT program test takers.* Princeton, NJ: Author.

EQUALS. (1986). *Cooperative geometry.* Berkeley, CA: Lawrence Hall of Science, University of California.

EQUALS. (1989). *Family math.* Portland, OR: Northwest EQUALS.

Gavin, M. K. (1996). The development of math talent: Influences on students at a women's college. *Journal of Secondary Gifted Education, 7,* 476–485.

Gavin, M. K. (1997). *A gender study of students with high mathematics ability: Personological, educational, and parental variables related to the intent to pursue quantitative fields of study.* Unpublished doctoral dissertation, University of Connecticut, Storrs.

Gavin, M. K., & Shmurak, C. B. (1999). *Learning together, learning apart: The effects of single sex mathematics classes in a coeducational school.* Paper presented at the American Educational Research Association Conference on Women and Education, Hofstra University, Uniondale, NY.

Gill, J. (1996). *Different contexts: Similar outcomes.* Paper presented at the annual meeting of the American Educational Research Association, New York.

Hanson, K. (1992). *Teaching mathematics effectively and equitably to females.* Newton, MA: WEEA Publishing Center/Center for Equity and Cultural Diversity.

Henry, J., & Manning, G. N. (1998). *Gender-based intervention making computer science appealing to girls in high school.* Unpublished master's inquiry project, University of Connecticut, Storrs.

Hernandez Garduño, E. L. (1997). *Effects of teaching problem solving through cooperative learning methods on student mathematics achievement, attitudes toward mathematics, mathematics self-efficacy, and metacognition.* Unpublished doctoral dissertation, University of Connecticut, Storrs.

Karp, K. S. & Niemi, R. C. (2000). The math club for girls and other problem solvers. *Mathematics Teaching in the Middle School, 5,* 426–432.

Kimball, M. M. (1989). A new perspective on women's math achievement. *Psychological Bulletin, 105,* 198–214.

Kissane, B. V. (1986). Selection of mathematically talented students. *Educational Studies in Mathematics, 17,* 221–241.

Kramer, P. E., & Lehman, S. (1990). Mismeasuring women: A critique research on computer ability and avoidance. *Signs: Journal of Women in Culture and Society, 16*(1), 158–172.

Lappan, G., Fey, J. T., Fitzgerald, W. M., Friel, S. N., and Phillips, E. D. (1998). *Ruins of Montarek: Spatial visualization.* White Plains, NY: Dale Seymour.

Learning Technology Center. (1996). *The adventures of Jasper Woodbury.* Mahwah, NJ: Erlbaum.

Leroux, J. A., & Ho, C. (1994). Success and mathematically gifted female students: The challenge continues. *Feminist Teacher, 7* (2), 42–48.

Linn, M. C., & Kessel, C. (1995). *Participation in mathematics courses and careers: Climate, grades, and entrance examination scores.* Paper presented at the Annual Meeting of the American Education Research Association, San Francisco, CA.

Martin, C. D., & Murchie-Beyma, E. (1992). *In search of gender free paradigms for computer science education.* (ERIC Document Reproduction Service No. ED 349 941)

National Council of Teachers of Mathematics (1992). *Data analysis and statistics across the curriculum.* Reston, VA: Author.

National Council of Teachers of Mathematics (2000). *Principles and standards for school mathematics.* Reston, VA: Author.

National Research Council. (1989). *Everybody counts: A report to the nation on the future of mathematics education.* Washington, DC: National Academy Press.

National Science Foundation. (1992). *Women and minorities in science and engineering: An update.* Washington, DC: Author.

National Science Foundation. (1996, September). *Women, minorities, and persons with disabilities in science and engineering.* Arlington, VA: Author.

Nelson, C. S., & Watson, J. A. (1991). The computer gender gap: Children's attitudes, performance, and socialization. *Journal of Education Technology Systems, 19,* 343–353.

Peterson, P. L., & Fennema, E. (1985). Effective teaching, student engagement in classroom activities, and sex-related differences in learning mathematics. *American Educational Research Journal, 22,* 309–335.

Reis, S. M. (1987). We can't change what we don't recognize: Understanding the special needs of gifted females. *Gifted Child Quarterly, 31,* 83–88.

Reis, S. M., & Callahan, C. M. (1989). Gifted females: They've come a long way—or have they? *Journal for the Education of the Gifted, 12,* 99-117.

Renzulli, J. S. (1977). *The enrichment triad model.* Mansfield Center, CT: Creative Learning Press.

Renzulli, J. S. (1994). *Schools for talent development: A practical plan for total school improvement.* Mansfield, CT: Creative Learning Press.

Rogers, P. (1990). Thoughts on power and pedagogy. In Leone Burton (Ed.), *Gender and mathematics: An international perspective* (pp. 38–46). London: Cassell.

Rosser, P. F. (1989). *Sex bias in college admissions tests: Why women lose out.* Cambridge, MA: National Center for Fair and Open Testing.

Sanders, J. S. (1994). *Bibliography on gender equity in mathematics, science, and technology: Resources for classroom teachers.* New York: Gender Equity Program, Center for Advanced Study in Education, CUNY Graduate Center.

Siegle, D., & Reis, S. M. (1994). Gender differences in teacher and student perceptions of student ability and effort. *Journal of Secondary Gifted Education, 6,* 86–92.

Streitmatter, Janice. (1997). An exploratory study of risk-taking and attitudes in a girls-only middle school math class. *Elementary School Journal, 98,* 15–26.

U.S. Bureau of Census. (1999). *Current population reports.* Washington, DC: Author.

Volman, M. (1997). Gender-related effects of computer and information literacy education. *Journal of Curriculum Studies,* 315–328.

Volpe, B. J. (1999). A girls' Math Olympiad team. *Mathematics Teaching in the Middle School, 4(5),* 290–293.

Wellesley College Center for Research on Women. (1992). *The AAUW report: How schools shortchange girls.* Washington, DC: American Association of University Women.

Wellesley College Center for Research on Women. (1998). *Gender gaps: Where schools still fail our children.* Washington, DC: American Association of University Women.

Wellesley College Center for Research on Women. (1998). *Separated by sex: A critical look at single-sex education for girls.* Washington, DC: American Association of University Women.

Wellesley College Center for Research on Women (2000). *Tech-Savvy: Educating girls in the new computer age.* Washington, DC: American Association of University Women.

Author Note

Portions of this chapter have been excerpted or paraphrased from *Work Left Undone: Choices & Compromises of Talented Females,* by S. M. Reis, 1998, Mansfield Center, CT: Creative Learning Press. Copyright ©1998 by Creative Learning Press. Used with permission.

appendix

Resources for Gifted Girls in Math and Science

compiled by **M. Katherine Gavin** *and* **Sally M. Reis**

Annotated List of Web Sites

Web Sites Focusing on Mathematics and Mathematically Talented Students

ENC Online (http://enc.org)

Eisenhower National Clearinghouse (ENC) is a repository for current mathematics and science resources. The site is a consistent award winner because it is well maintained and packed to the roof with math and science information. The sites include lessons, activities, interactive Web sites, and journal articles. The site links browsers to Digital Dozen (13 of the best-of-the-best science and mathematics sites, selected each month), Innovator of the Month (a spotlight on educators who are re-inventing learning with their students), ENC Focus (select resources for teaching current, hot topics), Lessons & Activities (Web sites to either supplement existing curricula or integrate into the classroom), among others. Absolutely top-shelf!

The Math Forum Home Page
(http://forum.swarthmore.edu)

This site is one of the most comprehensive resources for math teachers, students, and parents. One of the options, Ask Dr. Math, is a project allowing students to send in personal math questions and get personal answers. During the academic year, the "math doctors," undergraduate math majors at Swarthmore College, are available to communicate with K–12 students on math problems. Professors are also available. A weekly electronic newsletter is also available on the site as well as ideas for lesson plans, projects, problems of the day, and connections to other useful sites.

TERC (http://www.terc.edu)

TERC is a not-for-profit education and research and development organization dedicated to improving mathematics and science learning. Their Web site contains links to TERC projects in which students can get involved, as well as TERC papers, which explore a variety of innovative instructional strategies related to math and science teaching. A most notable link takes browsers to *Hands-On,* a magazine devoted to applying hands-on, inquiry-based learning to classrooms. The practical down-to-earth articles written by practitioners are inspirational and easy to adapt.

National Council of Teachers of Mathematics
(http://www.nctm.org)

This Web site contains the NCTM Principles and Standards for School Mathematics, as well as resources, lessons, and activities for elementary, middle, and high school students.

Fibonacci Numbers and the Golden Section
(http://www.mcs.surrey.ac.uk/Personal/R.Knott/
Fibonacci/fib.html)

This is an award-winning site that contains more than 200 pages of information about Fibonacci numbers and the Golden section and Golden string. Categories of information include: Fibonacci numbers and Golden sections in nature, the puzzling world of Fibonacci numbers, the intriguing mathematical world of Fibonacci and Phi, the Golden string, applications of Fibonacci numbers and Phi, and resources and links.

Web Sites Dealing Specifically With Gender Issues in Mathematics, Science, and Technology

Exploring Your Future in Math and Science: Encouraging Women in the Sciences (http://www.cs.wisc.edu/~karavan/afl/home.html)

This site explores why women are less likely to enter professions in math and science and offers information on salaries for math/science-related careers. It also offers information on how to start a math club for girls. Extensive links to resources for women in math and science make it possible to participate in e-mail discussion groups on gender issues.

Biographies of Women Mathematicians (http://www.agnesscott.edu/lriddle/women/women.htm)

This site provides extensive biographical information on women mathematicians, as well as some photos.

Women in Math Project (http://darkwing.uoregon.edu/~wmnmath)

This site provides an extensive collection of links to associations of interest to women in mathematics and links to data on the role of women in mathematics.

Girls: Math and Science Achievement (http://www.maec.org/girlmath.html)

This site provides information on math and science achievement for girls.

Closing the Gap: Math Clubs for Girls
(http://www.terc.edu/mathequity/cg/html/cg-home.html)

This Web site provides extensive information on using math clubs for girls.

Mathematics Contests and Competitions

American Mathematics Competitions
Dr. Walter E. Mientka, Executive Director
Department of Mathematics and Statistics
University of Nebraska
Lincoln, NE 68588-0658.

MathCounts
National Society of Professional Engineers Information Center
1420 King St.
Alexandria, VA 22314.

Mathematical Olympiad for Elementary Schools
125 Merle Ave.
Oceanside, NY 11572
(516) 781-2400

Mathematically Precocious Youth Program
Duke University Talent Identification Program
Box 40077
Durham, NC 27706-1742.

Dr. Luciano Corazza
Johns Hopkins University
2701 N. Charles St.
Baltimore, MD 21218.

Mathematics Pentathlon
P.O. Box 20590
Indianapolis, IN 46220.

National Mathematics League
P.O. Box 9459
Coral Springs, FL 33075.

Young Scholars Program
National Science Foundation
1800 G St. NW
Washington, DC 20550.

Annotated List of Teaching Resources

Cook. M. (1990). *Team estimation and analysis.* Balboa Island, CA: Marcy Cook.

This workbook is a series of group estimation activities integrating social studies and mathematical computation and concepts. Using a series of mathematical clues, teams work together to predict numerical information on historical or geographical topics. The final clues guarantee success—a really positive cooperative learning experience for the entire class in grades 4–8.

Downie, D., Slesnick, T., & Stenmark, J. K. (1981). *Math for girls and other problem solvers.* Berkeley, CA: Lawrence Hall of Science, University of California.

This book presents fun and challenging math activities. Topics explored include logic strategies and patterns, creative thinking, estimation, observation, spatial visualization, and careers.

Erickson, T. (1989). *Get it together.* Palo Alto, CA: Dale Seymour.
Erickson, T. (1996). *United we solve.* Oakland, CA: eeps media.

These books outline activities for groups using manipulatives ranging from pattern blocks to M&M's and toothpicks. Problems have a wide range of topics and difficulty, but all have the same format: six clue cards that together provide the information needed to solve the problem. Everyone in a group must work together because each member has different information needed for the solution.

Fraser, S. (1982). *Spaces: Solving problems of access to careers in engineering and science.* Palo Alto, CA: Dale Seymour.

The activities in *Spaces* were designed to stimulate students' curiosity and interest in doing mathematics. The classroom-tested lessons develop problem-solving skills and logical reasoning, build familiarity with mechanical tools, strengthen spatial visualization skills, and teach the importance of mathematics for opening occupational doors.

Franklin, Margaret. *Add-Ventures for girls: Building math confidence.* Newton, MA: WEEA Publishing Center.

This book combines teacher development with strategies that work in teaching mathematics to girls. It includes a chapter on computer equity issues that gives a list of questions for schools and/or teachers to assess the computer-learning climate for girls. (Available from the Women's Educational Equity Act Publishing Center, 55 Chapel St., Newton, MA 02160.)

Skolnick, J., Langbort, C., & Day, L. (1982). *How to encourage girls in math & science.* Palo Alto, CA: Dale Seymour.

This book focuses on ways to help girls acquire the skills and confidence they need to pursue a full range of interests in mathematics and science. It includes strategies and activities for developing spatial visualization, working with numbers, logical reasoning, and scientific investigation.

Other Teaching Resources

Gruver, N., & Kelly, J. (Eds.). *New moon: The magazine for girls and their dreams.* Duluth, MN: New Moon.

Karp, K., Brown, E. T., Allen, L., & Allen, C. (1998). *Feisty females: Inspiring girls to think mathematically.* Portsmouth, NH: Heinemann.

Lappan, G., Fey, J. T., Fitzgerald, W. M., Friel, S. N., & Phillips, E. D. (1998). *Ruins of Montarek: Spatial visualization.* White Plains, NY: Dale Seymour.

Learning Technology Center. (1996). *The adventures of Jasper Woodbury.* Mahwah, NJ: Erlbaum.

National Council of Teachers of Mathematics (1992). *Data analysis and statistics across the curriculum.* Reston, VA: Author.

National Council of Teachers of Mathematics. (2000). *Principles and standards for school mathematics.* Reston, VA: Author.

Perl, T. (1978). *Math equals.* Menlo Park, CA: Addison-Wesley.

Sanders, J. S. (1994). *Lifting the barriers: 600 strategies that really work to increase girls' participation in science, mathematics, and computers.* Port Washington, NY: Author.

Sanders, J., Koch, J., & Urso, J. (1997). *Gender equity right from the start: Instructional activities for teacher educators in mathematics, science, and technology.* Mahwah, NJ: Erlbaum.

Sanders, J., Koch, J., & Urso, J. (1997). *Gender equity sources and resources for education students.* Mahwah, NJ: Erlbaum.

Stenmark, J. K., Thompson, V. H., & Cossey, R. (1986). *Family math.* Berkeley, CA: Lawrence Hall of Science, University of California.

Resources on Notable Women

Cooney, M. (1996). *Celebrating women in mathematics and science.* Reston, VA: National Council of Teachers of Mathematics.

This book features 22 biographies of notable female mathematicians and scientists and shows how their determination, creativity, and intellectual passion helped them excel in their fields. Appropriate for use at the middle and high school levels, this book supplies many references that can be used for history of mathematics courses and is filled with excellent illustrations similar to woodcuts.

Edeen, S., Edeen, J., & Slachman, V. (1990). *Portraits for classroom bulletin boards: Women mathematicians.* Palo Alto, CA: Dale Seymour.

This kit is a set of black-line drawings (8" x 11") of 15 pioneering mathematicians with accompanying one-page biographies for quick bulletin boards or student handouts.

Perl, T. (1993). *Women and numbers: Lives of women mathematicians plus discovery activities.* San Carlos, CA: World Wide Publishing/Tetra.

This multicultural book relates the biographies of 13 outstanding mathematicians from the 19th and 20th centuries, examining where and how these women's interests in mathematics originated and their accomplishments in their chosen fields. It also includes enjoyable activities based on each woman's contributions to mathematics.

Organizations

Association for Women in Mathematics
University of Maryland
College Park, MD
http://www.awm-math.org

EQUALS
Lawrence Hall of Science
University of California, Berkeley
http://www.lawrencehallofscience.org/equals

Math/Science Network
http://www.expandingyourhorizons.org

National Women's History Project
(707) 636-2888
http://www.nwhp.org

SummerMath
Mount Holyoke College
(413) 538-2608
http://www.mtholyoke.edu/proj/summermath

About the Authors

M. Katherine Gavin is an associate professor at the Neag Center for Gifted Education and Talent Development at the University of Connecticut, where she serves as the math specialist in gifted education.

Eleanor Hall was a counseling psychologist at the Masterpeace Center for Counseling and Development in Tecumseh, MI. She passed away in January 2003.

Jan B. Hansen is assistant professor at the University of St. Thomas, School of Education in Minneapolis MN, where she teaches psychology and science.

Thomas P. Hébert is an associate professor of educational psychology in the College of Education at The University of Georgia in Athens, where he teaches graduate courses in gifted education. He is a member of the board of directors of the National Association for Gifted Children (NAGC).

Jennifer L. Jolly is a professional educator, consultant, and researcher who specializes in gifted education with an emphasis in the history of gifted education.

Linda A. Long teaches undergraduate and graduate courses in the School of Social Work at the University of Georgia and is in practice at Samaritan Counseling Services, where she specializes the social and emotional needs of academically gifted and talented children, adolescents, and their families.

Juanita Jo Matkins is a wife, mommy, and assistant professor of science education at the College of William & Mary in Williamsburg, VA.

Rhea Miles is an assistant professor in the Department of Mathematics and Science Education at East Carolina University.

Sally M. Reis is a professor and head of the Department of Educational Psychology at the University of Connecticut. She is also principal investigator for the National Research Center on the Gifted and Talented.

Leigh A. Rolnicki is an assistant professor in the Division of Counseling and Family Therapy at the University of Missouri at St. Louis. In addition to being a counselor educator, she is a licensed professional counselor (LPC) and has a private therapy and consulting practice in St. Louis County.

Julianne Jacob Ryan is a mental health counselor and a school social worker, specializing in the needs of the gifted and talented.

Kristie L. Speirs Neumeister is an assistant professor at Ball State University, where she teaches undergraduate psychology courses to preservice teachers and graduate courses in gifted education. Her research interests include the psychosocial issues facing gifted students.

Printed in the United States
by Baker & Taylor Publisher Services

Printed in the United States
by Baker & Taylor Publisher Services